Easy

Windows
troubleshooting

Other Computer Titles

by

Robert Penfold

Other Windows Titles

Easy Windows troubleshooting

Robert Penfold

Bernard Babani (publishing) Ltd
The Grampians
Shepherds Bush Road
London W6 7NF
England
www.babanibooks.com

Please note

Although every care has been taken with the production of this book to ensure that any projects, designs, modifications, and/or programs, etc., contained herewith, operate in a correct and safe manner and also that any components specified are normally available in Great Britain, the Publisher and Author do not accept responsibility in any way for the failure (including fault in design) of any projects, design, modification, or program to work correctly or to cause damage to any equipment that it may be connected to or used in conjunction with, or in respect of any other damage or injury that may be caused, nor do the Publishers accept responsibility in any way for the failure to obtain specified components.

Notice is also given that if any equipment that is still under warranty is modified in any way or used or connected with home-built equipment then that warranty may be void.

© 2001 BERNARD BABANI (publishing) LTD

First Published - March 2001

British Library Cataloguing in Publication Data
A catalogue record for this book is available from the British Library

ISBN   0 85934 495 9

Cover Design by Gregor Arthur
Printed and bound in Great Britain by Cox & Wyman

Preface

Although the Windows 95, 98, and Me operating systems are widely regarded as having a lack of stability, this reputation is not entirely fair. Software as complex as any version of Windows is never likely to be fully debugged, but it is not really any built-in bugs that are the major problem with Windows. It is the alterations that are made to the operating system after the basic installation process has been completed. The operating system is added to and altered each time any hardware or major piece of software is added or removed. Windows can be used with an enormous range of software and hardware, but this leaves it vulnerable to problems that originate in hardware drivers, installation programs, and uninstallers. Applications programs can also introduce difficulties if they do not strictly abide by the rules involving memory management, file naming, etc.

Ideally the user would install Windows and some applications programs, and then make no further changes to the system. For most users this is not practical though, and new hardware has to be added, software upgrades have to be installed from time to time, and so on. Most modern PCs tend to evolve over a period of time, and the operating system has to change to accommodate this evolution. If Windows should cease working it is not usually too difficult to get it up and running again. Most faults introduced into the system are easily reversed, provided you know how. This book details some simple procedures that enable most Windows faults to be quickly pinpointed and rectified. You do not have to be a computer expert in order to follow these procedures, but you do have to be familiar with the basics of using the Windows user interface.

Where a Windows installation becomes seriously damaged it may not be practical to repair it. Even if numerous files have been corrupted or deleted it is probably possible to repair the installation given enough time, but the more sensible approach is to reinstall the operating system. Full instructions for reinstalling Windows are provided, including reinstallation over an existing version and the "from scratch" approach. Either option may seem to be a rather daunting prospect for those of limited experience at Windows troubleshooting, but reinstalling Windows is not particularly difficult. It is the guaranteed method of curing Windows problems and getting your PC back in full working order again.

Robert Penfold

WARNING

*Sensible safety precautions should always be observed when dealing with electrical and electronic equipment, particularly any equipment that connects to the mains supply or operates at high voltages. **Do not open the case of a monitor or a PC power supply unit.** Apart from the fact that both of these are mains powered, they operate using high voltages that can remain on the circuit boards even after the equipment has been switched off for some time. If you use a PC connected to the mains supply as an earth for anti-static purposes, make sure that the power is switched off at the mains outlet so that the PC can not be accidentally switched on. With an AT case and power supply, examine the connections to the on/off switch before connecting the unit to the mains supply. All four connections should be completely covered by plastic insulators. **Do not use the unit if there are any signs at all of problems with the insulation.** Never work on a PC while it is switched on.*

Trademarks

Microsoft, MS/DOS, Windows, Windows Me, Windows 98 and Windows 95 are either registered trademarks or trademarks of Microsoft Corporation.

All other brand and product names used in this book are recognised trademarks, or registered trademarks of their respective companies. There is no intent to use any trademarks generically and readers should investigate ownership of a trademark before using it for any purpose.

Contents

3

Data rescue 85

4

Backup and restore 125

5

Reinstallation 161

Prevention is...

Causes

An installation of the Windows operating system coming to grief is not exactly a rare occurrence, but why should these problems happen at all? I suppose that the chances of removing every single bug from software as complex as this is virtually nil, but genuine bugs in Windows are almost certainly responsible for only a small percentage of the problems. Modern PC hardware is very reliable, and hardware glitches probably have nothing to do with the vast majority of problems either. Most of the difficulties seem to be due to things that either the user or applications programs do to Windows.

Unfortunately, quite minor things can prevent Windows from operating correctly, and it is easily "gummed up" by users making alterations to system settings or deleting essential files. Software that does not strictly abide by the rules can also generate problems. Probably the only sure-fire way of preventing Windows from getting into difficulties is to never install any applications programs at all, which is not exactly a practical proposition. However, you can certainly reduce the risk of problems occurring by following some simple rules.

Do not tweak

Experienced users fiddle around with the Windows configuration files and manage to customise the user interface in ways that are not normally possible. This is fine for those having suitable experience of Windows, because they know what they are doing. They can largely avoid problems and can soon backtrack to safety if something should go wrong. Inexperienced users are almost certain to damage the operating system if they try this sort of tweaking, and will not have the expertise to quickly sort things out when problems arise. Just the opposite in fact, and one thing can lead to another, with the operating system soon getting beyond redemption.

If you are not an expert on the inner workings of Windows it is best not to delve into its configuration files. A great deal of customisation can be done using the normal Windows facilities, and there are applications programs that enable further customisation to be undertaken without having to directly alter files.

Careful deletion

In the days of MS/DOS it was perfectly acceptable to delete a program and any files associated with it if you no longer wished to use the program. Matters are very different with Windows 95/98/Me, where most software is installed into the operating system. There are actually some simple programs that have just one file, and which do no require any installation. These standalone program files are quite rare these days, but they can be used much like old MS/DOS programs. To use the program you copy it onto the hard disc, and to run it you use the Run option from the Start menu, or locate the file using Windows Explorer and double-click on it. No installation program is used, and it is perfectly all right to remove the program by deleting the program file.

Most programs are installed onto the computer using an installation program, and this program does not simply make folders on the hard disc and copy files into them from the CD-ROM. It will also make changes to the Windows configuration files so that the program is properly integrated with the operating system. If you simply delete the program's directory structure to get rid of it, Windows will not be aware that the program has been removed. During the boot-up process the operating system will probably look for files associated with the deleted program, and will produce error messages when it fails to find them.

There is another potential problem in that Windows utilizes shared files. This is where one file, such as a DLL type, is shared by two or more programs. In deleting a program and the other files in its directory structure you could also be deleting files needed by other programs. This could prevent other programs from working properly, or even from starting up at all.

If a program is loaded onto the hard disc using an installation program, the only safe way of removing it is to use an uninstaller program. There are three possible ways of handling this.

Custom uninstaller

Some programs load an uninstaller program onto the hard disc as part of the installation process. This program is then available via the Start menu if you choose Programs, and then the name of the program concerned. When you choose this option there will be the program itself, plus at least one additional option in the sub-menu that appears. If there is no uninstall option here, no custom uninstaller has been installed for that program. Uninstaller programs of this type are almost invariably automatic in operation, so you have to do little more than instruct it to go ahead with the removal of the program.

With any uninstaller software you may be asked if certain files should be removed. This mostly occurs where the program finds shared files that no longer appear to be shared. In days gone by it did no seem to matter whether you opted to remove or leave these files, with Windows failing to work properly thereafter! These days things seem to be more reliable, and it is reasonably safe to accept either option. To leave the files in place is certainly the safest option, but it also results in files and possibly folders being left on the disc unnecessarily.

Windows uninstaller

Windows has a built-in uninstaller that can be accessed via the control panel. From the Start menu select Settings, Control Panel and Add/ Remove programs. By default this takes you to the uninstaller, and the lower section of the screen shows a list of the programs that can be uninstalled via this route (Figure 1.1). In theory the list should include all programs that have been added to the hard disc using an installation program. In practice there may be one or two that have not been installed "by the book" and can not be removed using this method. Some programs can only be removed using their own uninstaller program, while others have no means of removal at all. It is mainly older software that falls into the non-removable category, particularly programs that were written for Windows 3.1 and not one of the 32-bit versions of Windows. In fact it is very unusual for old Windows 3.1 software to have any means of removal.

Third party

There are uninstaller programs available that can be used to monitor an installation and then uninstall the software at some later time. As this feature is built into Windows 95/98/Me, and the vast majority of

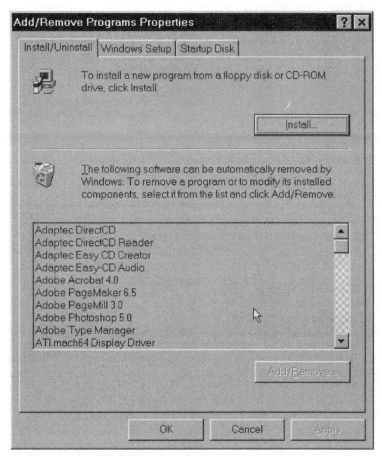

Fig.1.1 The built-in Windows uninstaller

applications programs now either utilize the built-in facility or have their own uninstaller software, these programs are perhaps less useful than they once were. Most will also assist in the removal of programs that they have not been used to install, and this is perhaps the more useful role. Most will also help with the removal of things like unwanted entries in the Start menu and act as general cleanup software, although Windows itself provides means of clearing some of this software debris. Figure 1.2 shows the CyberMedia Uninstaller program in action, but there are numerous programs of this type to choose from.

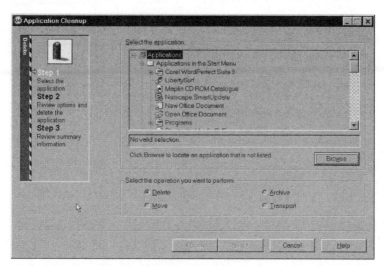

Fig.1.2 The CyberMedia uninstaller in action

Leftovers

Having removed a program by whatever means, you will sometimes find that there are still some files and folders associated with the program remaining on the hard disc. In some cases the remaining files are simply data or configuration files that have been generated while you were trying out the program. If they are no longer of any use to you there should be no problems if they are deleted using Windows Explorer. In other cases the files could be system files that the uninstaller has decided not to remove in case they are needed by other applications. Removing files of this type is more risky and it is probably better to leave them in place.

Sometimes the folders may seem to be empty, but it is best to check carefully before removing them. An important point to bear in mind here is that not all files are shown when using the default settings of Windows Explorer. Using the default settings hidden files will live up to their name and files having certain extensions are not shown either. In normal use this can be helpful because it results in files that are likely to be of interest being shown, while those that are of no interest are hidden. This makes it much easier to find the files you require in a folder that contains large numbers of files. It is not helpful when Windows troubleshooting because it tends to have the opposite effect to normal. Things like data files that are of little interest are shown, while many of

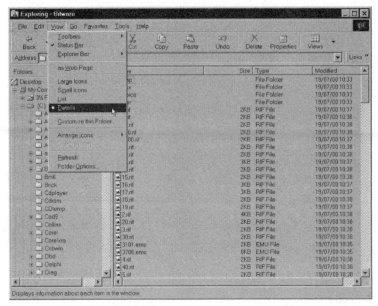

Fig.1.3 Windows can be set to show details for each file listed

the system files that are of interest are hidden. Windows Explorer should be set to show as much detail about the files as possible.

First go to the View menu and select the Details option (Figure 1.3). This will result in the size, type, and date of each file being shown. Then go to the View menu again, select Folder Options, and then left-click on the View tab in the new Window that appears (Figure 1.4). Under the Hidden Files entry in the main section of the window select the "Show all files" option. The hidden files are certain critical system files, such as those associated with the Windows Registry, that are not normally displayed by Windows Explorer so that they can not be accidentally altered or erased by the user. I would recommend ticking the checkbox for "Display full path in title bar". This way you can always see exactly what folder you are investigating, even if it is one that is buried deep in a complex directory structure.

Remove the tick in the checkbox next to "Hide the extension for known file types". The extension should then be shown for all file types, which makes it easy to see which one is which when several files have the same main file name. When viewing the contents of directories you can use either the List or Details options under the View menu, but the Details

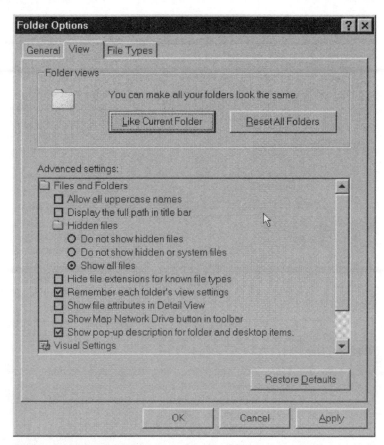

Fig.1.4 Windows Explorer can be made to show all file types

option provides a little more information. It provides the file type if it is a recognised type, and the date that the file was created or last altered. If the "Show attributes in Detail view" checkbox is ticked, it will also show the attribute of the file. These are the letters used for each of the four attributes:

A   Archive

H   Hidden

R   Read-only

S   System

Fig.1.5 An example file properties window

Thus a file that has "R" as its attribute letter it is a read-only type, and one that has "HA" in the attribute column is a hidden archive file. Choose the List option if you prefer to have as many files as possible listed on the screen. Details of any file listed can be obtained by right-clicking on its entry in Windows Explorer and then choosing the Properties option from the pop-up menu. This will bring up a screen of the type shown in Figure 1.5, which shows the type of file, the creation date, when it was last modified, size, etc.

Make sure that the checkbox for the "Remember each folder's view settings" is not ticked. Placing a tick in this box gives each folder its own settings, making it necessary to alter the settings for individual folders rather than altering them globally.

If any folders are definitely empty, there should be no problem if they are removed. The same is true of data and configuration files that are no longer needed. With other files it may not be clear what their exact purpose is, and it is a bit risky removing files of unknown function. Unfortunately, it is not uncommon for uninstallers to leave large numbers of files on the hard disc. The uninstaller seems to go through its routine in standard fashion, and reports that the program has been fully removed, but an inspection of the hard disc reveals that a vast directory structure remains.

I have encountered uninstallers that have left more than 50 megabytes of files on the disc, removing only about 10% of those initially installed. Other uninstallers report that some files and folders could not be removed, and that they must be dealt with manually. Some uninstallers seem to concentrate on extricating the program from the operating system by removing references to the program in the Windows registry, etc., rather than trying to remove all trace of it from the hard disc.

Softly, softly

So what do you do if the disc is left containing vast numbers of unwanted files after a program has been uninstalled? The temptation, and what many people actually do, is to simple drag the whole lot into the Recycle Bin. Sometimes this may be acceptable, but there is the risk that sooner or later Windows will look for some of the deleted files and start to produce error messages. If you are lucky, the deleted files will still be in the Recycle Bin, and they can then be restored to their original locations on the hard disc. If not, you may have problems sorting things out.

The safer way of handling things is to leave the directory structure and files intact, but change some file or folder names. If only a few files have been left behind, try adding a letter at the front of each filename. For example, a file called "drawprog.dll" could be renamed "zdrawprog.dll". This will prevent Windows from finding the file if it should be needed for some reason, but it is an easy matter for you to correct things by removing the "z" from the filename if problems occur. If there are numerous files in a complex directory structure to deal with it is not practical to rename all the individual files. Instead, the name of the highest folder in the directory structure is renamed. This should make it impossible for Windows to find the file unless it does a complete search of the hard disc, and it is easily reversed if problems should occur.

Ideally the complete directory structure should be copied to a mass storage device such as a CD writer, a backup hard disc drive, or another partition on the hard disc. The original structure can then be deleted. If problems occur and some of the files have been cleaned from the Recycle Bin, you can reinstate everything from the backup copy.

Modern hard disc drives have very high capacities so it is perhaps worthwhile considering whether it is really necessary to remove leftover files. If you do not need the hard disc space they can be left in place, avoiding the risks involved if they are removed. Do you really need to uninstall the program at all? The less installing and uninstalling you do the better the chances of avoiding problems. Eventually you will end up with a large number of installed programs and this could generally slow the system down. In particular, the boot-up process can become a very long and drawn out process. However, this can be overcome by wiping the hard disc clean and reinstalling the operating system and applications software from scratch. This is not a particularly quick and easy process, but it is the only totally reliable method of getting Windows back to a lean installation that operates at peak efficiency.

Icon and menu entries

After uninstalling a program you will often find that the shortcut icon is still present on the Windows desktop. If the installation program did not put the icon there in the first place it will not remove it. Shortcut icons that are placed on the Windows desktop manually must be removed manually. This simply entails dragging the icon to the Recycle Bin. There is no risk of this having an adverse effect on Windows operation.

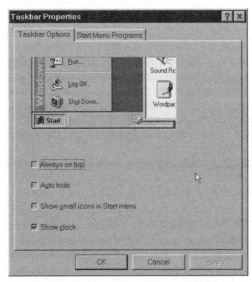

Fig.1.6 The Taskbar Properties window

An uninstaller should remove the entry in the Programs section of the Start menu when removing a program. Unfortunately, this item does sometimes seem to be overlooked, and after removing a number of programs there can be a growing band of orphan entries in the menu. Once again, removing these entries manually should not entail any risk of "gumming up" Windows.

To remove an entry go to the Settings entry in the Start menu, and then select Taskbar And Start Menu. This brings up the Window shown in Figure 1.6. The Taskbar menu is offered by default, so left-click the Start Menu tab to bring up the Window of Figure 1.7. Next left-click on the Remove button, which will bring up a scrollable list of all the items in the Start menu. Left-click on the item you wish to remove in order to highlight it (Figure 1.8), and then left-click the Remove button. A warning message will appear onscreen to give you a chance to change your mind, and the entry will be deleted if you confirm that you wish to go ahead. A quick check of the Start menu should show that the offending entry has been removed. It is actually placed in the Recycle Bin, so it can be easily reinstated if you make a mistake.

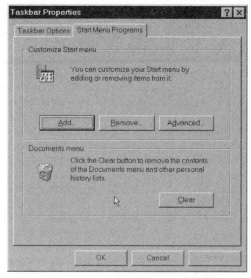

Fig.1.7 The Start Menu Programs screen

Old and new

Both old and brand new software are potential sources of problems with Windows. In the case of brand new software it is the beta test versions or any other versions prior to the commercial release that are the main problem. These are not fully tried and tested, and can not be guaranteed to do things "by the book". People who make a living testing this type of software almost invariably use one PC

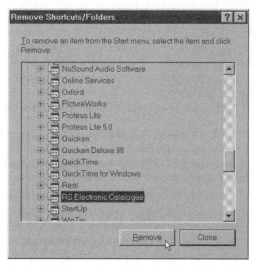

Fig.1.8 Selecting a menu entry for removal

for testing the software and a second PC for other purposes. That way there is no major loss if the test software runs amok and deletes half the files on the hard disc. If you do not have a second PC for use with dubious software it is best not to try it at all.

At one time the initial commercial releases of programs were not always reliable, and some software publishers seemed to be guilty of getting their customers to unwittingly do the final testing for them. This sort of thing may still go on in some niche markets, but it is thankfully something of a rarity these days. The cost of sending out replacement discs plus the loss of reputation makes it an unsustainable tactic. New software, whether it is totally new or an upgrade version should be very reliable these days. In the past it was advisable to let new software mature before buying it, but this should no longer be necessary. If new software should prove troublesome there should be a help-line that can give advice on the problem. Software publishers' web sites often have software patches that can fix any obscure problems that have come to light after the final versions of the programs have been sent out to the shops.

Memory

In the early days of Windows 95 it was not unusual for the dreaded red cross to appear on the screen complete with a brief error message. In fact there seemed to be one or two of these messages every time someone used a PC. Thankfully, this type of thing is relatively rare these days. There were probably two main reasons for these early problems, and one of them was a lack of memory in the PCs of the day. At that time memory was quite expensive. 8 megabytes of RAM was quite typical, and 16 megabytes was considered to be a large amount of RAM. Software manufacturers were eager for their programs to appeal to as many people as possible, which often led them to be overoptimistic about the system requirements. If the requirements listed 8 megabytes of memory as the minimum and recommended at least 16 megabytes should be used, then 16 megabytes was probably the minimum that would really give trouble free and usable results.

These days memory is relatively cheap, and PCs are mostly well endowed in this respect. On the other hand, programs seem to require ever more memory. Also, many users now have two or more programs running simultaneously, possibly with some background tasks running as well. If you run memory hungry programs on a computer that has a modest amount of memory and error messages keep on appearing, it is worth investing in some extra memory. Even if it does not cure the problem, Windows and your programs will almost certainly run more quickly.

The other problem in the early days of Windows 95 was that most Windows applications software was designed to work under Windows 3.1 and not Windows 95. Maybe in theory the programs should have run perfectly well, but in practice things did not always go well. In fact with some programs you were lucky to get to the end of the installation procedure without problems! Some of this software altered system files in a way that was permissible with MS/DOS and Windows 3.1, but was not the approved way of doing things with Windows 95 and later versions of Windows.

32-bit versions of Windows definitely work best with programs that are specifically written for use with them. Wherever possible use modern applications software and avoid the older programs. Apart from anything else, if you get into problems with software that is about five or more years old, it is unlikely that the software publisher will be eager to offer much help in getting it to run properly. It is by no means certain that the software publisher will still be in existence. Mergers, take-overs, and failures are not exactly unknown in the software world. Where there is no alternative to an old program you have little option but to use it and hope for the best. One precaution I would recommend is to copy the config.sys and autoexec.bat files onto a floppy disc before installing the vintage software. They can then be reinstated if there are boot problems after the program has been installed.

Windows problem?

Some users tend to jump to conclusions when there are problems with a PC running Windows. Probably most problems are the result of the operating system becoming damaged, but by no means all problems are caused in this way. I have often been asked to help with supposed Windows problems that turn out to be due to some other cause. A crucial consideration when locating the cause of a PC fault is where in the proceedings is it that things go awry? If the PC fails to start up at all, with no initial messages, etc., from the BIOS's POST (power-on self-test) program, the fault is clearly nothing to do with a Windows problem. The fault is occurring long before the PC starts to boot into Windows, and is presumably due to a hardware problem.

Matters are less clear cut if the PC gets through its initial checking, starts to boot into Windows, but rapidly comes to a halt. When this happens there will often be an error message along the lines that the boot disc is missing or has a corrupted boot sector, and you will be asked to insert a system disc and then press any key. This means that the computer has looked at the boot drives specified in the BIOS Setup program but has not found a bootable disc. An obvious first step is to check the BIOS settings by going into the Setup program. The manual for your computer should give at least brief details of how to enter the BIOS and change the settings. This is also covered in more detail in chapter 4. Assuming the settings are suitable, the problem could be due to hardware fault with the disc or the IDE interface on the motherboard, or it could be caused by corruption of the data in the boot sector of the disc.

Sometimes the PC will start booting, but it will stop almost immediately. When this happens there will not necessarily be an error message displayed on the screen. In fact there will probably be no message, with the computer instead "freezing". The Control-Alt-Del key combination might reset the computer so that it tries to boot again, but a hardware reset will probably be needed. In other words, operate the reset button on the computer if it has one, or switch off, wait a few seconds, and then switch the PC back on again. If the boot process almost instantly falters again it is possible that there is a hardware fault, but a corrupted boot sector on the disc is the most likely cause of the problem.

System files

If the system files in the boot sector of the disc have become damaged, the obvious first step is to replace them. In order to do this the computer should be booted using the Windows Startup disc in drive A:. A Startup disc is normally made during the Windows installation process, but one can also be made by selecting Settings from the Start menu, and then choosing Control Panel and Add/Remove Programs (Figure 1.9). Next operate the Startup Disk tab on the Window that appears, and follow the onscreen prompts. Note that the Windows installation disc will be required during the creation of the Startup disc, as will a 1.44-megabyte (formatted or unformatted) floppy disc.

Of course, if you can not boot the PC into Windows it is not possible to make the Startup disc this way, so make sure you have one of these discs available before trouble strikes. If you do get "caught short", one option is to find a friend who has a PC running the same version of Windows that you are using, and use their PC to make a Startup disc. In fact I would recommend having two Startup discs available, so that you can try the second disc if the PC fails to boot from the first one.

With Windows 98 there is another option provided the PC can be booted in MS/DOS mode with CD-ROM support. Whether or not the PC boots with CD-ROM support depends on the way it has been set up, but the

PC should really be supplied with the necessary drivers. Once booted in MS/DOS mode, set the CD-ROM drive as the current one, type this command, and press the Return key:

cd tools\mtsutil\fat32ebd

Next place a formatted 1.44-megabyte disc in drive A:, then type this command and press the Return key:

fat32ebd

Type "Y" to confirm that you wish to proceed, and the files will then be transferred to the floppy disc. Albeit very slowly, this process produces what seems to be a more or less normal Windows 98 Startup disc, complete with CD-ROM support. The disc contains the utility programs such as Scandisk, but it does not produce a virtual disc. It is intended as a means of producing a virus-free boot disc having FAT32 support, but it can presumably be used as a general-purpose emergency boot disc.

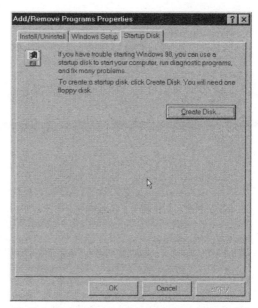

Fig.1.9 Creating a Windows Startup disc

First boot

With most PCs the BIOS is set so that the PC tries to boot from drive A: first, and then the hard disc (drive C:), so the computer should boot from drive A: without any problems. If not, check that the appropriate BIOS parameter has drive A: as the initial boot device, and change it if necessary. It is virtually certain that there is a hardware problem if the PC will not boot from floppy disc or from the hard disc drive.

Assuming you can get the computer booted using the Startup disc, the basic System files can be replaced on the hard disc. Booting from the Startup disc results in the creation of a virtual disc in the computer's memory, and this contains the program needed to replace the system files. In the drive letter sequence the virtual disc is normally placed between the hard disc and the CD-ROM drive. If there is a single hard disc with one partition, this will be drive C:, the virtual disc will be drive D:, and the CD-ROM will be drive E:. With two hard disc drives or one drive having two partitions, the virtual and CD-ROM drives will be moved up by one letter, becoming drives E: and F:. For the sake of this example we will assume that there is one hard disc drive with a single partition, and that the virtual disc is drive D:.

First make the virtual disc the current drive by typing "D:" and pressing the Return key. Then type "dir" and press the Return key, which should bring up an onscreen list of the files on drive D:. One of these is "sys.com", the program needed to replace the system files. This program will only work if the system is on the default drive, so type "A:" to go back into drive A:, and then type this command to place the system files onto drive C::

E:\sys C:

After pressing the return key the program will immediately start copying the files from the floppy disc onto the hard disc. Assuming all goes well a "System Transferred" message will appear on the screen. Remove the Startup disc from drive A: and then press the Control, Alt, and Delete key together to reset the PC. With luck it will boot properly into Windows. At the very least the boot process should get further than it did previously, and with Windows 95 and 98 installations it should be possible to boot the computer in MS/DOS mode. This is not possible with Windows Me because the appropriate menu option is absent when the F8 function key is pressed at the start of the boot-up process. However, it may be possible to boot the computer in Safe mode even if this was not possible previously.

Reinstalling the basic system files will sometimes permit Windows to load again, but it is only fair to point out that it will fail to totally cure the problem in the majority of cases. All sys.com does is to reinstall the MS/DOS system files, and it does not repair any of the Windows system files. If the PC still fails to boot properly into Windows it is a matter of delving further into the problem using the techniques described in chapter 2. If there is wholesale damage to the Windows files it may be a matter of reinstalling Windows. In an extreme case any important data on the hard disc that has not been backed up must be rescued, and then the hard disc wiped clean so that Windows can be installed "from scratch". Emergency rescue of data, backing up the hard disc, and reinstalling Windows are covered in chapters 3, 4, and 5.

Late problems

Sometimes Windows seems to get 90 percent of the way through the boot-up process before it comes to a halt. When this happens it is likely that the problem is in the Windows installation and not due to a hardware fault. When things come to a halt with an error message stating that a certain file or files could not be found, this indicates that the problem is within Windows itself. Matters are less clear cut if any error messages refer to an item of hardware, or Windows tries to reinstall an item of hardware that was previously installed correctly. It could be that the trouble is due to problems with a corrupted driver program, but it is also possible that a faulty item of hardware is giving the Windows Plug and Play facility some difficulties.

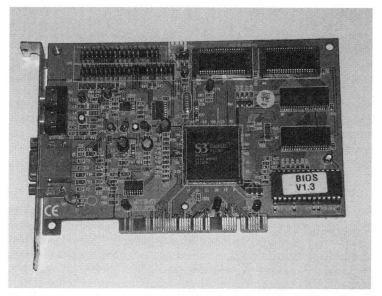

Fig.1.10 A typical expansion card. The mounting bracket is on the left

On the cards

Fixing hardware problems goes beyond the scope of this book, but it is covered in "Easy PC troubleshooting (BP484)" from the same publisher and author as this book. However, if the item of hardware that seems to be giving problems is an expansion card, it is probably worthwhile checking that it is properly seated in its expansion slot. To do this you will have to remove either the outer casing or a side panel, depending on the style of case used for your PC. An expansion card has a metal bracket that is used to secure it to the rear of the PC's chassis, and connections on the bottom edge that fit into the expansion slot. The metal bracket can be seen at the left end of the card shown in Figure 1.10, and the connections can be seen on the extended part of the card at the bottom.

To remove the card the fixing bolt on the mounting bracket must be removed (Figure 1.11), and then the card can be pulled free. Many PC expansion cards are vulnerable to damage from static charges, even those charges of modest voltage, so a certain amount of care must be exercised when pulling the card free of the expansion slot. In this case things are eased by the fact that the card does not need to be completely removed from the PC. It is just a matter of pulling the card free of the expansion slot and then pushing it firmly back into position again. This makes sure that the card is fully pushed down into place in its slot.

Fig.1.11 An expansion card ready for removal Removing   and

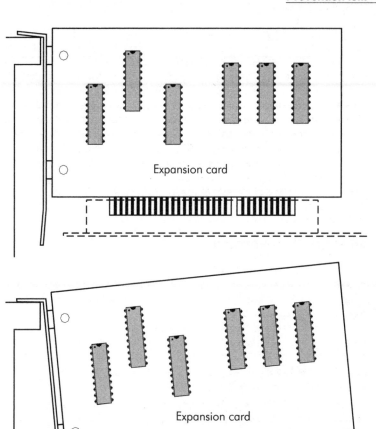

Fig.1.12 An expansion card can cause problems if its mounting bracket does not have the correct right-angled bend

replacing the card also tends to clean the connectors so that any connections that were previously a bit iffy make good contact once more.

In order to avoid damage from static charge it is advisable to leave the PC connected to the mains supply, but to switch it off at both the mains socket and the PC's on/off switch. Although the PC is switched off it will be earthed to the mains earth connection. Touch the metal chassis of the chassis before pulling the card from its slot. This will remove any static charge in your body and should be sufficient to ensure that no harm comes to any of the PC's hardware. Make sure that the card is parallel to the slot as in the upper view of Figure 1.12, and not at an angle to it as in the lower view. The bend at the top of the mounting bracket is often something less than a perfect right angle, which tends to skew the card slightly as the fixing bolt is screwed into place. Therefore, make quite sure that the card stays parallel to the expansion slot when the card is fixed in place. If necessary, remove the card again and carefully bend the top of the bracket to produce a better approximation to a right angle.

Diagnostics software

Diagnostics software intended to help to locate the source of a hardware problem can be useful if you are unsure if a problem is due to an obscure Windows fault or an intermittent hardware problem. Suppose you have a PC that is largely working but seems to be a bit erratic or unreliable. Perhaps it sometimes boots into Windows all right but it hangs up on other occasions. Once into Windows, things may go perfectly well for a few minutes and then the computer suddenly crashes. This sort of thing can be caused by a software fault, but it is often due to something like a memory, processor, or disc problem.

If a problem only occurs when a certain applications program is run, the problem probably has its origins in that piece of software. Running hardware checks is then a little pointless, and it is matter of contacting the software publisher in search of a solution to the problem. Similarly, if the problem only occurs after a particular program has been used, it is very unlikely that either Windows or a hardware fault is the cause of the problem. It is again a matter of contacting the software publisher to see if there is a known problem with the applications program.

You may have some hardware diagnostics software, and if so it is certainly worthwhile running the software on a PC that is giving intermittent problems. In my experience, if a PC has a tendency to simply grind to a halt with the display freezing, the problem is more likely to be in the hardware than the software. This is also the case where things come to a halt with the screen going blank. The fault is more likely to be in the software if the dreaded Windows error messages ("This program has performed an illegal operation and will shut down", etc.) keep appearing. However, this is only a general rule and there are exceptions.

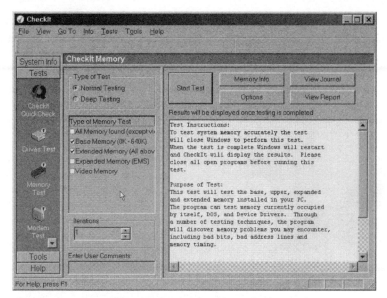

Fig.1.13 The Checkit memory test screen

Diagnostics programs will run tests on many parts of the system, including hard and floppy disc drives, the main memory, video memory, the processor, and the ports. Programs of this type sometimes operate under MS/DOS. This is primarily so that they can take control of the memory when making memory tests. Windows places restrictions on the way memory is allocated to programs, and would therefore place much of the memory beyond the reach of the diagnostics software. Even where diagnostics programs run under Windows, to make certain tests they will often reboot into MS/DOS to perform the tests, and then go back into Windows to display the results. Figure 1.13 shows the Checkit memory test screen, and Figure 1.14 shows an example set of test results after rebooting into MS/DOS and then back into Windows 98 again. This makes the testing rather longwinded, but it is perhaps a more convenient way of doing things than rebooting into MS/DOS and carrying out all the tests from there.

For those that prefer to use diagnostic programs from within MS/DOS rather than Windows there are still programs of this type available. In order to work properly a program of this type normally requires the PC to boot into a very basic MS/DOS environment that is free from any memory management programs or other software that runs in the

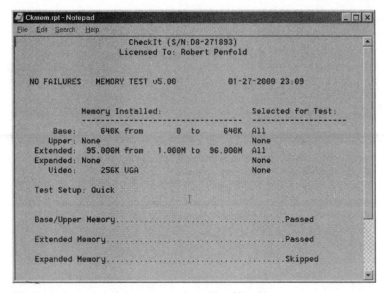

Fig.1.14 A test result screen produced by Checkit

background. Even things like mouse and CD-ROM drivers have to be avoided in most cases. The PC is therefore booted using a basic floppy boot disc produced using the Format command with the /s switch, or using sys.com to copy the system files onto an otherwise blank disc.

A Windows Startup disc loads various drivers and other programs during the boot process and is unlikely to be suitable as the boot disc when using diagnostics software. With Windows 95 and 98 it is possible to perform a very basic MS/DOS boot-up by pressing the F8 function key as Windows starts to load, and then selecting option 6 (Safe mode command prompt only) from the menu that appears. This option is not available with Windows Me incidentally. With some of these programs the PC must be booted using a custom boot disc, and the instruction manual should give details of how this disc is produced.

Once into a diagnostics program of this type things are not much different to a Windows equivalent. Control is via the keyboard rather than using the mouse, but is otherwise similar. The same kinds of test are available, as can be seen from the screen shot of Figure 1.15, which shows the main screen of Amidiag 5.4. Figure 1.16 shows the result of a processor test using this program.

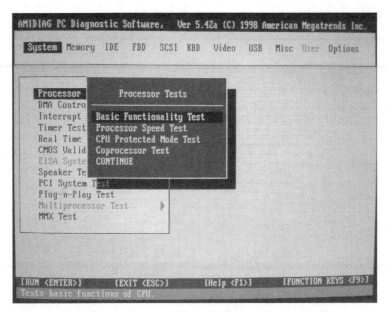

Fig.1.15 The main screen of the Amidiag diagnostics program

If a fault only occurs intermittently it might be necessary to repeat the test procedures a few times in order to coax the system into an error while the diagnostics software is running. Obviously you should try to concentrate on tests that are likely to bring results, and not bother too much about tests on parts of the system that are unlikely to be causing the problem. Faults associated with the ports and the floppy disc drive are unlikely to be responsible for bringing the system to a halt at times when none of these are in use. On the other hand, you may as well give every part of the system a "quick once over" while you are using the diagnostics software, just in case the problem does actually lie in an unlikely part of the system. If the system has a tendency to hang up periodically, the memory, processor and video card are probably the most likely sources of the problem.

What is a virus?

Do not overlook the possibility of problems being caused by a computer virus. There is actually a variety of program types that can attack a computer system and damage files on any accessible disc drive. These

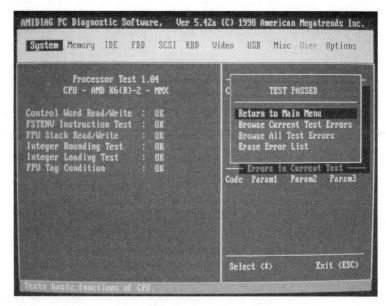

Fig.1.16 Processor test result produced by Amidiag

tend to be lumped together under the term "virus", but strictly speaking a virus is a parasitic program that can reproduce itself and spread across a system, or from one system to another. A virus attaches itself to other programs, but it is not immediately apparent to the user that anything has happened. A virus can be benign, but usually it starts to do serious damage at some stage, and will often infect the boot sector of the hard disc, rendering the system unbootable. It can also affect the FAT (file allocation table) of a disc so that the computer can not find some of the files stored on the disc. The partition table can also be affected, so that the reported size of a disc does not match up with its true capacity. The disc might even be rendered totally inaccessible. The less subtle viruses take more direct action such as attempting to erase or overwrite everything on the hard disc, or erasing the system files while flashing an abusive message on the screen.

A virus can be spread from one computer to another via an infected file, which can enter the second computer via a disc, a modem, or over a network. In fact any means of transferring a file from one computer to another is a potential route for spreading viruses. A program is really only a virus if it attaches itself to other programs and replicates itself. A program is not a virus if it is put forward as a useful applications program but it actually starts damaging the system when it is run. This type of program is more correctly called a "Trojan horse" or just a "Trojan". Either way, these programs can cause immense damage to the files on the disc, but there should be no risk of any hardware damage occurring.

Virus protection

This is a case where the old adage of "prevention is better than cure" certainly applies. There is probably a cure for every computer virus, but identifying and eradicating a virus can take a great deal of time. Also, having removed the virus there is no guarantee that all your files will still be intact. In fact there is a good chance that some damage will have been done. The ideal approach is to avoid doing anything that could introduce a virus into the system, but for most users this is not a practical proposition. These days computing is increasingly about communications between PCs and any swapping of data between PCs provides a route for the spread of viruses. It used to be said that PC viruses could only be spread via discs that contained programs, and that data discs posed no major threat. It is in fact possible for a virus to infect a PC from a data disc, but only if the disc is left in the drive and the computer tries to boot from it at switch-on.

These days there is another method for viruses to spread from data discs, and this is via macros contained within the data files. Obviously not all applications software supports macros, but it is as well to regard data discs as potential virus carriers. Some of the most widespread and harmful viruses in recent times have been propagated via Emails containing macros infected with a virus, so this problem is one that needs to be taken very seriously.

Given that it is not practical for most users to avoid any possible contact with computer viruses, the alternative is to rely on anti-virus software to deal with any viruses that do come along. Ideally one of the "big name" anti-virus programs should be installed on the system and it should then be kept up to date. This should ensure that any infected disc is soon spotted and dealt with. Software of this type is designed for use before any problems occur, and it normally runs in the background, checking any potential sources of infection as they appear. There is usually a direct mode as well, which enables discs, memory, etc., to be checked for viruses.

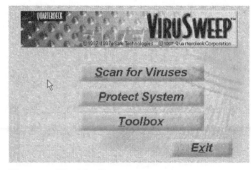

Fig.1.17 The ViruSweep start up screen

Figure 1.17 shows the start up screen for the Quarterdeck ViruSweep program, and selecting the "Scan For Viruses" option takes the user into further screens that permit various options to be selected. The first screen (Figure 1.18) permits the user to select the parts of the

Fig.1.18 The first ViruSweep screen when scanning for viruses

Fig.1.19 This screen enables the type of scan to be selected

system that will be checked. Viruses can exist in memory as well as in disc files, so checking the memory is normally an option. Further screens enable the type of scan to be selected (Figure 1.19), and the action to be taken if a virus is detected (Figure 1.20). Most anti-virus software has the option of removing a virus rather than simply indicating that it has been detected. Note though, that in some cases it might not be possible to automatically "kill" a virus. The program will then usually give details of how to manually remove the virus.

Things are likely to be very difficult if you do not use anti-virus software and your PC becomes infected. On the face of it, you can simply load an anti-virus program onto the hard disc and then use it to remove the virus. In practice it is definitely not advisable to try this method, and most software of this type will not load onto the hard disc if it detects that a virus is present. This may seem to greatly reduce the usefulness

Fig.1.20 This screen gives control over the action taken when a virus is detected

of the software, but there is a good reason for not loading any software onto an infected system. This is the risk of further spreading the virus by loading new software onto the computer. With a lot of new files loaded onto the hard disc there is plenty of opportunity for the virus to infect more files.

Most viruses can actually be removed once they have infected a system, but not usually by loading a major piece of anti-virus software onto the hard disc and using it to remove the virus. The method offered by many anti-virus suites is to boot from a special floppy disc that contains anti-virus software. With this method there is no need to load any software onto the hard disc, and consequently there is no risk of the anti-virus software causing the virus to be spread further over the system. With the Norton Anti-virus 2000 program a boot disc plus four support discs are made during the installation process (Figure 1.21). If boot problems

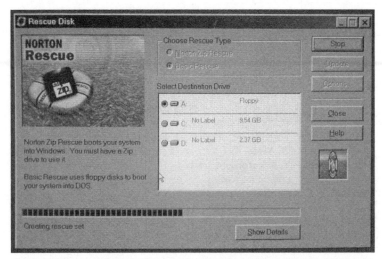

Fig.1.21 Most anti-virus programs can make recovery discs. Norton Anti-virus 2000 makes a set of five recovery discs

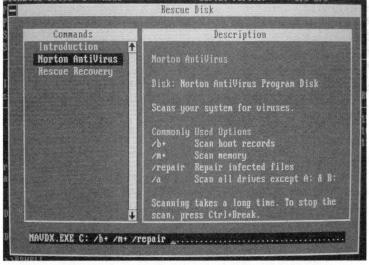

Fig.1.22 Virus scanning with the aid of the Norton Anti-virus 2000 recovery discs

occur at a later date, the PC can be booted using the Norton boot disc, and with the aid of the other discs a comprehensive range of virus scans can be undertaken (Figure 1.22). In some cases the virus can be removed automatically, and it might also be possible to have any damage to the system files repaired automatically as well.

Often it will soon become clear if a virus or similar program is the cause of Windows problems. The virus will proudly proclaim its presence with an onscreen message. In other cases it will not do so, making it difficult to determine whether the problem is due to a virus or a genuine problem with Windows. If there are repeated problems with the boot files becoming damaged or erased, it is very likely that a virus or similar program is responsible. A lot of inexplicable changes to the Windows Registry and other system or configuration files is also good grounds for suspicion.

If at first...

There is plenty of anti-virus software available commercially, on the Internet at low cost or free, and it is often given away on the cover-mounted CD-ROMs supplied with computer magazines. If you suspect there may be a virus causing the problem it is best to use at least two and preferably three up to date anti-virus programs to check the PC's hard disc. Where applicable, download updates for the software so that you are using the most up to date versions that should detect any new viruses. There is no guarantee that the problem is not due to a virus in the event that the programs fail to detect one. On the other hand, it becomes an outside chance and it is probably better to follow other avenues of investigation rather than pursue a virus that is probably not there.

It is only fair to point out that even if the anti-virus software does find a virus and kill it, you may still need to do some work in order to get the computer up and running again. The anti-virus program may be able to repair all the damage inflicted by the virus, but there is a fair chance that the damage will be too great for everything to be fixed. Anyway, with the virus killed off you are at least in a position to start repairing the damage and return things to normality.

Before continuing with this it is not a bad idea to give some thought to the way in which the virus found its way into your PC. There is otherwise a risk that it will soon return and undo the repairs you have made. If you had been using some discs from another computer prior to the problem occurring, check all those discs using the anti-virus programs. Bear in mind that many viruses have a sort of gestation period, and that there can be a substantial gap between the virus program finding its way into your PC and the program actually starting to do its worst. Ideally you should check all discs that have been used with the PC in the previous few weeks or even months.

Closing notes

It helps to avoid problems if the PC is closed down in the approved fashion at the end of each session. Simply switching off with Windows still running is unlikely to do any harm, but is certainly not a good idea. Switching off with applications programs running is worse, and can lead to problems with Windows or the applications programs. One potential cause of difficulties is that Windows itself and many applications programs place temporary files on the hard disc drive. When Windows and the applications programs are shut down in the correct manner

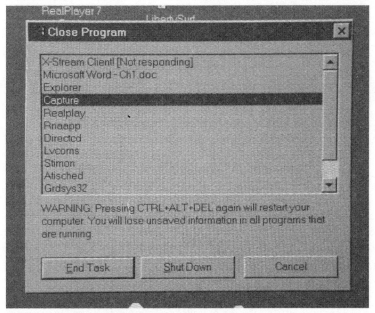

Fig.1.23 The Close Programs window, which can also be used to close Windows itself

these files are deleted. If you simply switch off with things still running, or the PC is suddenly switched off due to a power failure or hardware fault, these files are left on the disc. This may not matter, but there is a risk of the files confusing matters when the PC is switched on again.

Even if you do close down Windows correctly every time, it is still possible to run into difficulties with problem software. You are unlikely to use Windows for very long without encountering a program that either just "freezes" and does not respond to the mouse or keyboard. The more interesting variation is the program that starts to behave erratically with commands having the wrong effect, odd things happening on the screen, etc. Often when this occurs the program fails to close down when the cross icon in the top right-hand corner of the screen is operated. Once an application program has gone seriously awry it is not uncommon for Windows itself to behave erratically, and it will often fail to close down properly.

Wherever possible applications and Windows should be shut down properly, or in a reasonably orderly fashion, rather than simply resorting to the on/off switch or Reset button. Windows does provide an escape route that will usually do the trick if the PC becomes seriously "gummed up". With MS/DOS the Control-Alt-Delete key combination resets the computer, but it has a somewhat different effect in Windows 95/98/Me. Rather than immediately resetting the PC, a message appears on the screen, as in Figure 1.23. These four options are available:

1   Press Control-Alt-Delete again to reset the computer, which will then reboot

2   Operate the Cancel button to return to Windows without changing anything

3   Operate the End Task button to close the program that is highlighted in the program list

4   Operate the Shut Down button to shut down Windows

If an application program is proving troublesome and can not be shut down in the usual way, the third option offers a possible solution to the problem. You may well be puzzled at the number of programs in the list, since with Windows and a couple of applications programs running there could be half a dozen or more programs listed. The reason for the discrepancy is that modern PCs tend to have various background tasks running. In the list of Figure 1.23, amongst other things there is a screen capture program and the driver software for a CD-ROM writer. Explorer is effectively Windows itself incidentally, so if you close that program Windows will shut down.

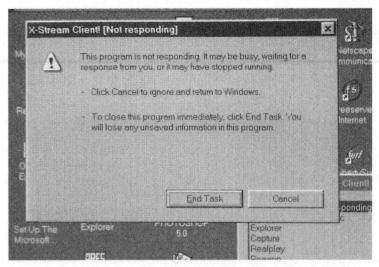

Fig.1.24 When this message appears it should finally be possible to close down the troublesome program

To close a program using this route, simply left-click on its entry in the program list and then operate the End Task button. This never seems to instantly shut down the program, and instead a further message appears on the screen (Figure 1.24). Note that this second message can appear within a couple of seconds, or it can take some time, so be patient and wait to see what happens. If you have made a mistake and chosen the wrong program, left-click on the Cancel button and then press Control-Alt-Delete again so that you can have another try. Operate the End Task button to close the program. Incidentally, this is not meant to be a normal method of closing a program, and should only be used in an emergency, or to close down a background task that can not be terminated in any other way.

The PC may operate normally once a troublesome program has been closed down. If so, I would not recommend simply carrying on as if nothing had happened. It is safer to save any unsaved data and close down any applications that are running. Then restart Windows and launch the applications programs again. This way you should manage to avoid any nasty surprises that the rogue application might have left behind.

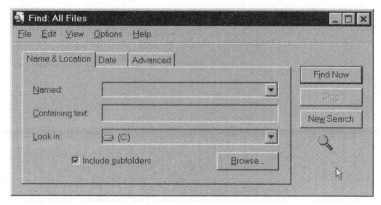

Fig.1.25 Using the Find Files or Folders facility of Windows Explorer

Emergency exit

Unfortunately, in situations where the crashed software has managed to get Windows seriously out of kilter it may not be possible to regain proper control. Where possible, save any unsaved data before trying to exit Windows. Try to close any running applications programs via the normal route first, or by way of the Control-Alt-Delete route if that proves to be impossible. Where possible Windows should be closed down via the Start menu in the normal fashion, but if this proves fruitless or impossible, try the Control-Alt-Delete method.

If the Shut Down button does not have the desired effect, press Control-Alt-Delete again to check for more programs that are not responding. If no crashed programs are reported, pressing Control-Alt-Delete again will probably reset the PC and get the system out of Windows. Another option is to start closing down the background tasks one by one in an attempt to regain proper control of the PC. It is quite likely that a fault in one of these programs is causing the problem, and by a process of elimination it should be possible to find the culprit.

If Windows has well and truly crashed, often the screen will freeze or the computer will ignore input from the keyboard or the mouse buttons. Another possibility is that you will find yourself going round in "ever decreasing circles" repeatedly closing down Windows without it actually closing down. In these situations it is probably not worthwhile trying to find an orderly exit route. It is quite likely that there is no tidy way of

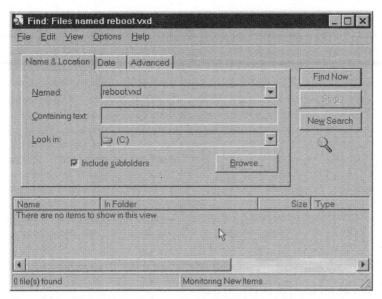

Fig.1.26 In this case the search proved fruitless, and another avenue of investigation had to be pursued

closing down Windows once things get this badly messed up. Simply press the reset button or switch the PC off, wait a few seconds, then switch it on again and hope.

Sometimes the Control-Alt-Delete combination will fail to bring up the Close Program window. This can be due to a surplus reboot.vxd file, and deleting the unnecessary file should solve the problem. Start by using Windows Explorer to search for files of this name. Go to the Tools menu and then select Find followed by Files or Folders. This will bring up a Window like the one shown in Figure 1.25. Enter "reboot.vxd" as the name of the file to search for, make sure that you are checking drive C: and that the "include subfolders" checkbox is ticked. Left-click the Find Now button and the program will search all the folders on drive C: for the file. It should not find it, giving a Window like Figure 1.26 once the search has been completed. If "reboot.vxd" is found, left-click on its entry to highlight it, and then either select Delete from the Edit menu or just press the Delete key.

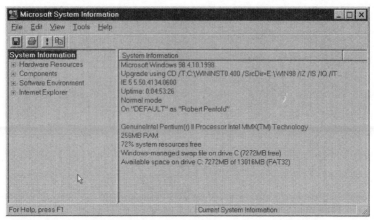

Fig.1.27 The Windows 98 System Information screen includes information about the amount of memory currently in use

Background information

As pointed out in the previous section, most modern PCs usually have a number of background tasks in operation, and not just Windows plus any applications you are running. If you use the Control-Alt-Delete immediately after a PC has booted into Windows you will probably find quite a list of programs, and not just Windows Explorer in the program list. Some of these programs are probably providing essential Windows functions, while others are drivers for complex pieces of hardware, anti-virus monitoring routines, etc.

In theory there should be no problem in having numerous background tasks provided the PC has enough memory to accommodate everything. In practice the PC might not have sufficient memory to accommodate all the programs if there is a large number of them and you use memory hungry applications. Also, if your PC has only the minimum recommended amount of memory for the version of Windows in use, having large numbers of background tasks is inviting problems. The appearance of error messages mentioning illegal operations, fatal exception errors, and page faults are often indicative of faulty memory or inadequate memory allied with poor memory management.

With any version of Windows 95, 98 or Me you can check the amount of free memory by running the System Information utility. From the Start

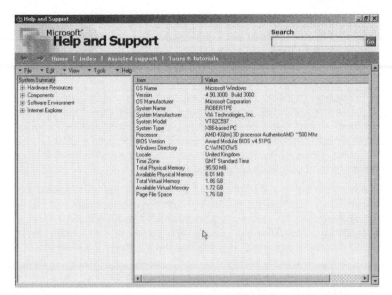

Fig.1.28 This is the Windows Me version of the system information screen

menu select Accessories, System Tools, and then System Information. The Windows 98 version of this utility is shown in operation in Figure 1.27. The important figure here is the one that gives the percentage of system resources that are free. In this example some 72 percent is free, which should give trouble-free operation.

Figure 1.28 shows the Windows Me equivalent, which does not present the information in quite the same way. The total physical memory is quoted, which is the amount of RAM fitted to the computer. This seems to be about 1 megabyte less than the amount of RAM actually installed, and I would guess that it does not include the lowest 1-megabyte which is used by MS/DOS but not by 32-bit versions of Windows. The virtual memory includes hard disc space that can be used as a sort of slow alternative to RAM. In the example of Figure 1.28 the PC has 95-megabytes of RAM, of which only about 6-megabytes are free. As things stand there is no major problem, but running another major application would seem to be out of the question.

Another potential problem is that of the background tasks proving to be incompatible. In theory this should not happen, but with something as complex as this there is always a chance of things going wrong, and in practice things will go wrong from time to time. The computer might simply "freeze", but a more likely outcome is that an error message will appear, probably explaining that a task has a fatal problem and that it will shut down.

With this type of thing it is easy to jump to conclusions that the program that has generated the error message is the one that is causing the problem. It can in fact be due to one program interfering with another program and causing it to crash. If a variety of programs suddenly have a tendency to crash it is likely that there is a problem in Windows itself or a background task is causing problems.

If a problem starts just after some new software has been added it is always likely that there is a problem with the new software. In cases where the new software includes a background task it is that much more likely that the new software is responsible for the system's instability. If problems occur after new software has been installed, it is worthwhile uninstalling the program to see if normality returns. When a new program does seem to be the culprit it is a matter of contacting the software publisher to see if they can offer any assistance. Some background tasks seem to be mutually incompatible, and you may have to opt for leaving one or other of them off the system.

System Tray

The System Tray, also known as "Systray" is at the bottom right corner of the main Windows screen, and here you will find icons for a number of background tasks, such as audio control panel, anti-virus software, etc., and the Windows clock. These programs, and probably a number of others, are launched as part of the Windows start-up routine. If you suspect that something here is giving problems, it is possible to stop the program from loading via the System Configuration utility. In order to start this utility select Programs from the Start menu, followed by System Tools and System Information. Then choose System Configuration Utility from the Tools menu and left-click on the Startup tab. This should produce a window something like Figure 1.29.

All the programs that run at start up are listed here, and there is a checkbox beside each one. Uncheck the box for any program that you do not wish to be launched at start up. Alternatively, if there is a program that should be launched at start up but it is failing to appear, make sure that it is in the list and that its checkbox is ticked. Some of the entries in

Fig.1.29 The System Configuration utility enables the user to decide which programs are run at start up

the list are sometimes a bit cryptic, but you should be able to find the ones you need. Note that some of the programs are part of Windows and not software you have added to the basic installation. For example, the Registry Checker utility is run each time Windows starts up. When you have finished, operate the Apply and OK buttons. You will then be asked if you would like to restart the computer. The changes will not take effect until Windows has rebooted.

Points to remember

Do not mess around with the Windows Registry or configuration files unless you know exactly what you are doing.

Do not delete files manually unless you are sure it is safe to remove them. Where possible, programs should be removed using their own uninstall utility or the built-in facility of Windows.

Avoid using any form of beta or test software. If you wish to experiment with software of dubious stability, have a PC specifically for this purpose. Try to avoid using old software that was not written for 32-bit versions of software. Modern software is safer and should run much better.

Do not blame Windows if things grind to a halt before the boot-up sequence starts. A failure this early in the start up sequence is due to a hardware fault or an error in the BIOS settings.

A hardware fault can be responsible for the boot-up process failing almost as soon as it starts, or never actually starting. However, it could be due to damaged or missing boot files, so try replacing them using the MS/DOS Sys program.

If you have access to some diagnostics software, use it to check that the problem is not due to a hardware fault. Make sure the expansion cards are fitted into their expansion slots correctly.

If the boot process stalls late in the boot sequence check that the hardware drivers are properly installed. One of the programs that runs at start up could also be the cause of the problem.

The fact that a virus has not announced its presence does not mean it is not there. If there are inexplicable problems with the system use anti-virus programs to scan the files on the hard disc, recently used floppy discs, etc. Ideally an anti-virus program should be installed on the PC and used to make regular checks of the system.

Do not switch off your PC while Windows is still running. Shut down Windows first, and then switch off your PC if it is a type that does not switch off automatically.

Even if the operating system or applications software are behaving abnormally, try to close down the system properly.

Do not get your computer to "bite off more than it can chew". There is a limit to the amount of software that a PC can have running at the same time. The operating system can be damaged if the computer keeps running out of resources and crashing.

Troubleshooting

Booting problems

Many users of MS/DOS were surprised at the ease with which the new operating system could be halted in its tracks when they moved to Windows 95. A relatively simple operating system such as MS/DOS does not usually fail to boot unless there is damage to one of the boot files. When things go wrong it will throw up a few error messages during the boot process, and it may not operate exactly as you would like once the system has booted, but the system will usually boot. Having booted, it will to a large extent be functioning and usable.

The situation is different with a complex operating systems such as Windows 95, 98, and Me which are dependent on numerous files being present and correct on the hard disc. If any one of these files is damaged or absent, or a configuration file erroneously specifies a file that is not present, the boot process will often stop about half way through the process. In fact quite minor problems seem to bring the boot process to a halt, such as the system running out of "environmental space", which seems to mean a lack of memory set aside for use as buffers, for use by the PATH command, etc.

Windows 95/98/Me do not operate under the "boot anyway" philosophy of MS/DOS. This cautious approach could be by accident rather than design, but it is probably a safety measure to ensure that the system only boots if it can do so reliably. With a more complex operating system such as Windows 95, 98, or Me the last thing you need is the system booting but then running amok.

Not all Windows problems centre on boot problems, but it is probably true to say that the vast majority do. Windows can boot normally and then give difficulties, but this is often the result of problems elsewhere in the system. Hardware faults and bugs in applications software can both produce this kind of behaviour. Much of this chapter is therefore devoted to boot problems, and it is this topic that is covered first.

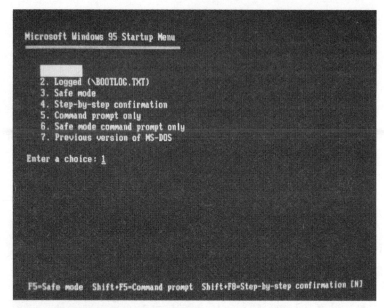

```
Microsoft Windows 95 Startup Menu


   ▮▮▮▮▮▮▮
   2. Logged (\BOOTLOG.TXT)
   3. Safe mode
   4. Step-by-step confirmation
   5. Command prompt only
   6. Safe mode command prompt only
   7. Previous version of MS-DOS

Enter a choice: 1




F5=Safe mode  Shift+F5=Command prompt  Shift+F8=Step-by-step confirmation [N]
```

Fig.2.1 The upgrade version of Windows 95 offers seven options

Safety first

Do not jump to the conclusion that the system has become unusable because Windows crashes during the boot-up sequence. There could be a major problem, but it is worth resetting the computer a couple of times to see if the problem clears itself. Also try switching off, waiting a few seconds, and then turning the PC on again. There can be an occasional problem with a piece of hardware failing to reset properly at switch-on. Switching the PC off and on again will usually clear this sort of problem. If that fails, boot in Safe mode (as described in the next part of this chapter), shut down Windows in the usual way, and then try rebooting normally.

When repeated attempts to boot the system result in the boot process coming to a premature end, Windows should be booted in Safe mode again. This is a sort of very basic "boot at all costs" mode that can be used when troubleshooting. There are other modes that can be useful when Windows troubleshooting. In order to boot into one of these modes the F8 function key must be pressed as soon as the BIOS start up routine ends and the boot process begins.

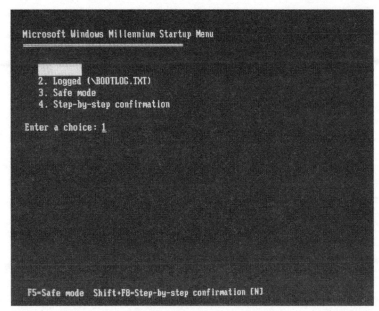

Microsoft Windows Millennium Startup Menu

2. Logged (\BOOTLOG.TXT)
3. Safe mode
4. Step-by-step confirmation

Enter a choice: 1

F5=Safe mode   Shift+F8=Step-by-step confirmation [N]

Fig.2.2 Windows Me offers just four start up options

There is only a very brief gap between the BIOS finishing its start up processes and the system starting to boot, so you must press F8 as soon as the BIOS has finished its routine. In fact with some systems the only reliable way of entering Safe mode is to repeatedly press F8 as the end of the start up routine approaches. Pressing F8 when using Windows 98 brings up the simple menu system shown here:

Microsoft Windows 98 Startup Menu

1.   Normal

2.   Logged (\BOOTLOG.TXT)

3.   Safe mode

4.   Step-by-step confirmation

5.   Command prompt only

6.   Safe mode command prompt only

In the mode

There is an additional option in the Windows 95 equivalent (Figure 2.1), but this only appears in the upgrade version. Windows Me has a much reduced set of options (Figure 2.2), and is more dependent on Safe mode than the other versions of Windows, so we will consider Windows Me separately. It is perhaps worth considering the various Windows 95 and 98 options before proceeding to consider Safe mode in detail.

1.   Normal

Booting using the Normal option takes the PC through a normal Windows boot-up process, but is obviously of no use if this process fails and the computer hangs up.

2.   Logged mode

Logged mode produces a normal boot sequence, but a log of the boot processes is placed in a text file on the boot drive. As we shall see later, this can be useful in determining the cause of a boot failure.

3.   Safe mode

Safe Mode boots into Windows, but only a minimalist version of the operating system. The display is a basic 640 by 480 pixel type using 16 colours, and items of hardware such as the soundcard, CD-ROM drive and modem will not be operational in this mode. Some of the Windows facilities either fail to operate at all or only work in a simplified mode. Because Safe Mode provides a very basic version of Windows it is usually possible to boot in this mode even if the Windows installation is badly damaged. Unfortunately, once into Safe mode it can sometimes be difficult to track down the cause of the problem and fix it due to the reduced functionality.

4.   Step-by-step confirmation

Using step-by-step confirmation means that Windows will ask the user for confirmation before processing configuration files, device drivers, etc. The point of this is that it enables parts of the boot process to be bypassed, and this can help to locate the cause of the problem. In many cases it can also help to get the PC booted into a version of Windows that has more functionality than Safe Mode, possibly making it easier to sort out the cause of the problem.

5. Command prompt only

The "Command prompt only" option boots the computer into the Windows 95 or 98 version of MS/DOS. Depending on how the PC is set up, this might get some of the hardware such as the CD-ROM drive and soundcard working, whereas they are left non-functioning in Safe Mode. However, when Windows fault finding it is often better to boot from drive A: using a Windows Startup disc rather than use this mode. The Startup disc provides some useful utility programs which are not necessarily available when booting into the Command prompt mode from drive C:.

6. Safe mode command prompt

Do not confuse option 3 (Safe Mode) with option 6 (Safe mode command prompt only). Using option 6 results in the PC booting into a very basic version of MS/DOS, with the autoexec.bat and config.sys files being ignored. One reason for using this mode is that the PC will always boot into MS/DOS provided the boot files are intact. Anything in the configuration files that causes the boot to fail will be ignored. It is unusual for an entry in the configuration files to prevent MS/DOS from booting, but it can occasionally happen. This is usually when a severe case of recursion results in the boot up process repeating something indefinitely. Another reason for using this mode is that some diagnostics and anti-virus software requires the PC to be booted into a "clean" version of MS/DOS having no drivers, etc., installed. This mode provides an easy way of booting into a completely "clean" version of MS/DOS.

7. Previous MS/DOS mode

As pointed out previously, option 7 is only provided when using the upgrade version of Windows 95. Normally this will have been installed on top of MS/DOS, and with this option it is possible to boot into the version of MS/DOS that was installed prior to the upgrade. This option is presumably included to make it easier to run MS/DOS applications software, and it is probably not of any value in the current context.

Using Safe mode

Select option three to boot the system in Safe mode, or simply use F5 rather than F8 to skip the menu and boot straight into this mode. As pointed out previously, booting the system in Safe mode will almost invariably get the PC into Windows, and the computer will be "up and running" to some extent. A warning message towards the end of the

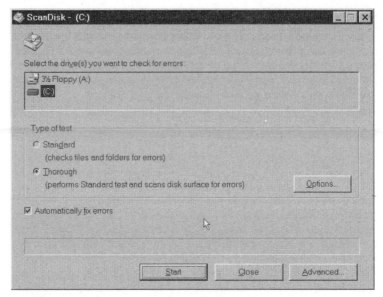

*Fig.2.3 Scandisk offers two basic modes of operation, which are
Standard and Thorough*

boot process explains that Safe mode provides a simplified version of
the operating system. It is only intended to permit problems with the
system to be traced and fixed, and it is not designed to permit the system
to be used normally. I suppose that in an emergency it might be possible
to run applications programs in Safe mode, but this is something that
should only done when suitably desperate.

One major difference between Safe mode and normal operation is the
lack of proper hardware support. The video card will of course function,
but only in a basic VGA mode. Exotic pieces of hardware will not function
because their drivers will not have been loaded, and even some basic
pieces of hardware such as the CD-ROM drive and the soundcard will
not function for the same reason. Provided the mouse is a reasonably
standard type is should still function in Safe mode. It is important to
realise that the lack of hardware support is not the only failing. Some of
the facilities provided by the operating system will also be lacking, which
is a pity because this can sometimes make life difficult when trying to
sort out a problem.

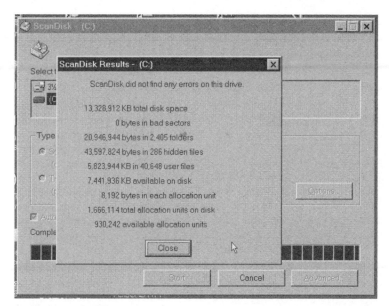

Fig.2.4 Scandisk provides a report once a scan has been completed

Basic checks

Once the PC is booted in Safe mode you can undertake some basic checks, and the usual starting point is the Windows Scandisk utility, which can be accessed from the Start menu by selecting Programs, Accessories, System Tools, and Scandisk. The Scandisk utility seems to be the much same in both Windows 95 and 98, and it offers two modes of operation. These are Standard and Thorough modes, and you operate the radio buttons to select the one you require (Figure 2.3).

The Standard check looks for irregularities in the file and folder structure. This includes simple things like filenames that do not adhere to the rules, and more serious problems such as one sector of the disc being assigned to two or more files. Program crashes can leave problems of these types, so it is not a bad idea to run Scandisk if a program comes to an unscheduled finish. If you tick the appropriate checkbox Scandisk will try to repair any errors that it finds.

Initially I would recommend using the Standard mode with the checkbox ticked. This test should be relatively fast, taking no more than a few

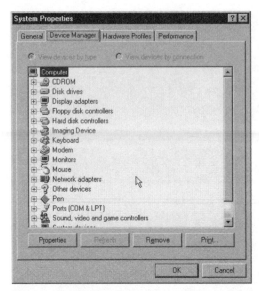

Fig.2.5 The System Properties screen

minutes. If the program discovers any problems it will report them via onscreen messages, and at the end it also gives a brief summary of its findings (Figure 2.4). Unfortunately, if Scandisk does find some errors and fixes them, this does not necessarily mean that the Windows will then boot perfectly. The problems will be fixed in the sense that filenames will adhere to the rules, linked files will be unlinked so that each sector of the disc is assigned to only one file, and so on. Any damaged files may not be fully restored using Scandisk. If one file partly overwrites another file there is no way that a utility program such as Scandisk can restore the overwritten part of the file. Unless you have a backup copy the damaged file will be lost permanently. However, Scandisk should at least restore order to the disc if things have gone wrong, improving the chances of getting things running smoothly again.

The Thorough mode performs the same tests as the Standard mode, but it additionally carries out a surface scan of the disc. In other words, it checks that there are no weak spots on the disc that are causing data to become corrupted. It is certainly worth using the Thorough mode if you suspect that the disc itself may be causing problems. Note though, that a thorough check of this type on a large hard disc drive will take quite a long time. It will probably take a few hours rather than a few minutes for the test to be completed.

Hardware drivers

Devices such as soundcards, video cards, and even the built-in interfaces of the PC such as the parallel and USB ports require drivers to integrate

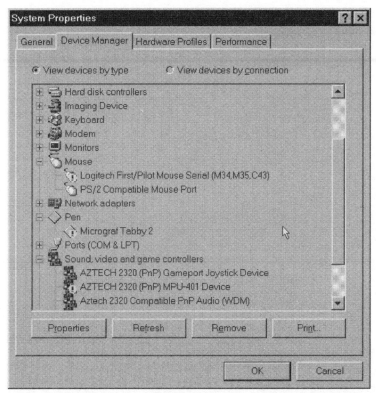

Fig.2.6 Device Manager uses yellow exclamation marks to indicate problems with items of hardware

them with the Windows operating system. Problems with Windows drivers are not exactly a rarity, and it is best to check for driver faults sooner rather than later. The normal way of doing this is to go into Device Manager. This can be run from the Start menu by selecting Settings, Control Panel, and then double clicking on the System icon. Left-click on the Device Manager tab of the window that appears, and you will then have a screen something like Figure 2.5.

Normally there will be a yellow exclamation mark (!) against an entry if the program has detected a problem with the item of hardware in that category. Double clicking on an entry in the table expands it to show all the drivers in that category and where appropriate there will be an exclamation mark against an entry (Figure 2.6). In fact Windows will

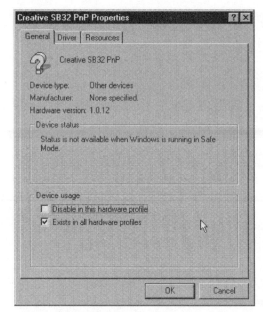

Fig.2.7 Device Manager can be less than forthcoming when used in Safe mode

usually expand a category for you if it contains an item of hardware that seems to have a problem. In normal operation it is possible to double-click on an entry that has a question or exclamation mark in order to get further details on the problem.

Unfortunately, in Safe mode Device Manager is not fully operational, and its diagnostic abilities are practically zero. Figures 2.5 and 2.6, which actually show the Device Manager for the same computer but running in Safe mode and Normal mode respectively, demonstrate this point. If you try to get status information in Safe mode you simply get a message of the type shown in Figure 2.7, explaining that status information is not available in Safe mode. In order to use Device Manager properly it is necessary to get the PC booted in normal mode, even if this means bypassing some parts of the boot-up process and having Windows less than fully operational for the time being. This can usually be achieved using the step-by-step confirmation method of booting, as described later in this chapter.

Old hardware

It is best not to jump to conclusions where the PC is one that has been in use for some time and it has undergone some changes to the hardware over the years. In the example of Figure 2.6 the faulty mouse is in fact one that had been removed long ago and replaced by a mouse port type. The driver for the old mouse had not been removed, but the PC worked properly because the drivers for the new mouse had been installed properly. This demonstrates the point that problems with hardware will not necessarily prevent Windows from booting. With things such as mice and soundcards the PC will often boot-up even if there is a problem, but the hardware concerned will not work properly. The drivers for more crucial items of hardware such as the hard disc drive and the video card are more likely to bring the boot process to a halt.

Where hardware problems are found in Device Manager it certainly makes sense to sort them out before trying to proceed further. This might get the system working properly again or there could still be boot problems, but it at least clears away some potential causes of the problem. Reinstalling drivers can be problematic with the old drivers still in place. Even though there is a suspected problem with the existing ones, Windows can be reluctant to replace them with drivers that do not have a later date.

It is best to remove the existing drivers and then shut down Windows and reboot the system. Drivers are easily removed using Device Manager, and it is just a matter of left clicking on the relevant entry to highlight it and then operating the Remove button. Left-click on the OK button when the warning message appears on the screen (Figure 2.8). The relevant entry should then disappear from the list of devices. Note that it is not possible to select and remove a category from the Device Manager list.

Where all the drivers in a category are giving problems they must be removed individually. Even where (say) just one out of four drivers for a soundcard is not working properly, it is best to remove all the drivers and reinstall everything "from scratch". The drivers can be reinstalled via Device Manager provided the system was not booted in Safe mode. If the system can only be booted in Safe mode it is worth trying the Add New Hardware option of the Control Panel, which usually seems to work in this mode. Note also that some hardware drivers have their own installation program and do not have to use the standard Windows methods. Before attempting to reinstall the drivers make sure you read the manufacturer's installation instructions.

If you have an Internet connection it is a good idea to check the manufacturer's web site to see if a more recent version of the driver software is available. There are usually frequent updates to the drivers for newer items of equipment. In general it is not a good idea to install an updated driver with the old version still in place, so use Device Manager to remove the original driver before installing the new one. One exception to this is where the updated driver is not actually a full set of driver software. Sometimes the new version uses some of the original

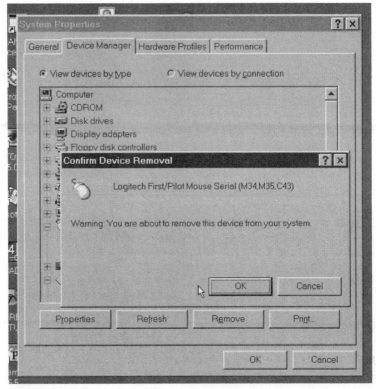

Fig.2.8 Device drivers are easily removed using Device Manager

files, while changing other files and (or) adding new ones. As always, read the installation instructions before installing the new software. This should state whether or not the original drivers should be left in place or removed. It is does not, then the old drivers should be removed prior to installing the new ones.

Hardware problems

If repeated reinstallation of the drivers fails to clear the yellow exclamation marks, and updated drivers do not help either, it is quite likely that the cause of the trouble is a hardware fault. In the case of an expansion card, check that it is fitted in its expansion slot using the simple method

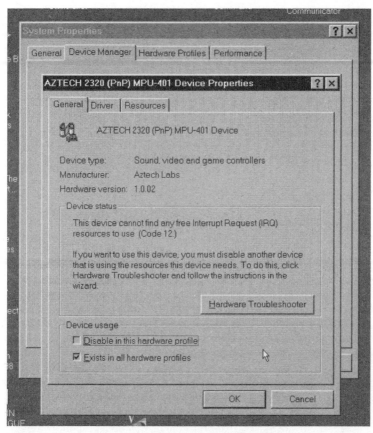

*Fig.2.9 When Windows is booted in Normal mode, Device Manager
will give some details of hardware or driver problems*

outlined in chapter 1. If the PC can be booted in normal mode, use
Device Manager to check the cause of the problem. Double-click on the
entry for the troublesome device to bring up a window like the one in
Figure 2.9. The program may be vague in its reporting of the fault,
stating something along the lines that the device is not working properly,
and that the hardware is faulty or the drivers are not installed.

In the example of Figure 2.9 it is quite specific, reporting that there is a
hardware conflict. In other words, this device needs to use resources of
the computer that are already used by another piece of hardware. A

problem of this type should not occur if the PC has been in use and working well for some time. It is more the type of thing that happens when new hardware is added to a PC. A hardware conflict is not strictly speaking a Windows problem, and goes beyond the scope of this book. Windows provides some built-in help for dealing with this type of thing in the form of the Hardware Troubleshooter. This can be launched by operating the Hardware Troubleshooter button in the Device Properties window. Wizards will then guide you through the process of sorting things out. With luck the problem will soon be cured, but if inadequate resources are available for all the hardware there will be no alternative to disabling one of the devices producing the conflict.

Logging

If no problems can be found with the hardware, or sorting out the problems that are found makes no different to the boot problems, it is time to look elsewhere for the fault. Newly installed software that makes a mess of a configuration file is probably the most common cause of Windows start up problems. If the system refuses to boot just after some new software has been installed it is odds-on that the installation program has made a mistake somewhere in the process. There are two options in the Windows 95/98 start up menu that help you to discover the root cause of the fault when the system refuses to boot. The first of these is option two, which provides a logged start up.

Depending on the way your PC is configured, it may provide a long string of messages detailing what is happening during the boot process, or it may suppress these messages. Even if these messages are displayed, on a modern PC you often find that many of them scroll off the screen so fast that there is little chance of reading them. The basic function of the logged boot up is to write these messages to a file called Bootlog.txt that is placed in the root directory of the boot disc. This file can be read using any text editor or word processor. Incidentally, the previous version of the file, if there is one, will be saved as Bootlog.prv.

One of Window's built-in text editors can be used to examine the Bootlog file if your PC is not equipped with a word processor. From the Start menu choose Programs, Accessories and then Wordpad. This produces a simple but effective word processor, and the Bootlog file can be loaded by selecting File and Open. This produces the standard Windows file requester that can be directed to the root directory of drive C:. Make sure that either text (txt) files (Figure 2.10) or all files (*.*) is selected in the lower part of the window, or Bootlog.txt will be "invisible" to the file requester.

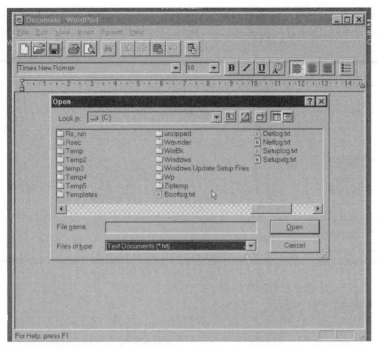

Fig.2.10 Make sure that the word processor is set to recognise a file having a "txt" extension

Once loaded, there is no difficulty in making a detailed examination of the file's contents. The list of messages is comprehensive and provides a full list of every action during boot up. The file also shows whether or not each action was successful. This is just a small sample from a long BOOTLOG file:

```
[00109EE9] Loading Device =
C:\WINDOWS\SETVER.EXE
[00109EE9] LoadSuccess    =
C:\WINDOWS\SETVER.EXE
[00109EE9] Loading Device =
C:\WINDOWS\COMMAND\ANSI.SYS
[00109EE9] LoadSuccess    =
```

```
C:\WINDOWS\COMMAND\ANSI.SYS
[00109EE9] Loading Device = C:\MTM\MTMCDAI.SYS
[00109F0B] LoadSuccess    = C:\MTM\MTMCDAI.SYS
[00109F0B] Loading Device =
C:\WAVRIDER\DRIVERS\SGIDECD.SYS
[00109F26] LoadFailed     =
C:\WAVRIDER\DRIVERS\SGIDECD.SYS
[00109F26] Loading Device =
C:\WINDOWS\COMMAND\DISPLAY.SYS
[00109F32] LoadSuccess    =
C:\WINDOWS\COMMAND\DISPLAY.SYS
[00109F32] Loading Device =
C:\WINDOWS\HIMeM.SYS
[00109F32] LoadSuccess    =
C:\WINDOWS\HIMeM.SYS
[00109F32] Loading Device =
C:\WINDOWS\DBLBUFF.SYS
[00109F32] LoadSuccess    =
C:\WINDOWS\DBLBUFF.SYS
[00109F32] Loading Device =
C:\WINDOWS\IFSHLP.SYS
[00109F32] LoadSuccess    =
C:\WINDOWS\IFSHLP.SYS
[00109F33] C:\COLOUR.EXE[00109F33]  starting
[00109F33]
C:\WINDOWS\COMMAND\MODE.COM[00109F34]  starting
[00109F33]
C:\WINDOWS\COMMAND\MODE.COM[00109F33]  starting
[00109F33] C:\WINDOWS\COMMAND\KEYB.COM(Logo
disabled)
[00109F33]   starting
[00109F45] C:\WINDOWS\AZTPNP.EXE[00109F45]
starting
[00109F56] C:\WINDOWS\AZTPNP.EXE[00109F56]
starting
```

As with all faultfinding, resist the temptation to jump to conclusions. In this list there is one line that failed, but it is obvious that this did not bring things to an immediate halt because the boot process continued on for dozens more lines and processes. The system file (SGIDECD.SYS) that failed to load is a driver for a soundcard no longer fitted to the system. The required file was no longer on the system, and was no longer needed. Its failure to load was ignored by the system, which continued to boot. Most Boot.log files seem to show a few failed processes that turn out to be of no consequence. It is conceivable that an error early in the proceedings could result in failure later in the boot process, but it is towards the end of the Bootlog file that the cause of the problem is most likely to be found.

Step-by-step

Option four in the Windows start up menu provides an alternative method of locating the problem, and is the one I would recommend using. Step-by-step confirmation, as one would expect from its name, means that the system will go through the boot process step-by-step, and that it will only include those steps that the user authorises. This enables the user to see exactly where things grind to a halt, and with further attempts it is possible to bypass certain stages of the boot process to see if this enables the system to boot. Note that this method of booting offers the option of having a Boot.log file generated. It is a good idea to select this option. You may not need the Boot.log file, but it will be there if it should be required.

It is often helpful to try booting the computer without the config.sys file being processed, or if that does not get the system to boot try again without the autoexec.bat file being processed. If blocking one of these enables the system to boot, examine the relevant file (which will be in the root directory of the boot drive) using a word processor or text editor. When editing any configuration file it is necessary to take great care not to make inadvertent changes to the file. If you are not very careful you could easily end up doing more harm than good. Always save an unchanged version of the file to provide a backup if you make a mess of things and need to return to the original version of the file. I recommend making a backup on the hard drive called something like config.bak or autoexec.bak, and also making a backup copy on a floppy disc which should be write protected so that it can not be accidentally overwritten.

If you wish to get rid of a line in the file that seems to be causing the problem, a useful ploy is to add "Rem" followed by a space at the beginning of that line. This tells the operating system to ignore the line because it contains a remark that is merely there as an aid to anyone examining the file. The advantage of this method over deleting the line is that it is so easy to put things back the way they were. If you need to reinstate the line you simply delete the four characters you added. There is little chance of accidentally altering the line, because you never make any changes to the original text. It is worth looking for repetition in these configuration files.

Some installation programs make automatic changes to configuration files, and things do not always work quite as they should. For example, you will often find two or three almost identical PATH commands in the autoexec.bat file. What seems to happen is that an installation program adds a new PATH command that is the same as the original except that it has one or two additions at the end. Presumably the original PATH command is supposed to be erased, but a flaw in the installation program leaves it intact.

The same sort of thing can happen with other commands. The additional commands may seem to be of no consequence, but they will take up memory, and the memory set aside for this purpose may be used up. This usually produce error messages along the lines "not enough environment space". Lines in the configuration files that run drivers that are no longer necessary or undertake any unnecessary operations can waste memory and prevent the system from booting properly. Strangely perhaps, MS/DOS problems that prevent Windows from booting will not necessarily prevent MS/DOS from booting. Hence it is sometimes possible to boot into MS/DOS, type "win" and press the Return key, and launch Windows successfully, even though booting directly into Windows is not possible.

As can be seem from the screen shot of Figure 2.11, if you opt to have the config.sys or autoexec.bat file processed at boot-up, you then have control over the individual lines of each file. If the problem does exist in either of the MS/DOS configuration files, by a process of elimination this method should enable the exact cause of the problem to be located.

Later problems

If Windows stalls quite late in the boot sequence it is unlikely that the processing of the MS/DOS configuration files is causing the problem. In this case you should opt to have the Windows Registry processed during boot-up and to have the Windows graphical user interface installed. Initially try loading everything on offer until the boot process comes to a halt. The last boot process prior to the system hanging-up is probably the one that is causing the problem, but it could conceivably be something earlier on that is causing the problem.

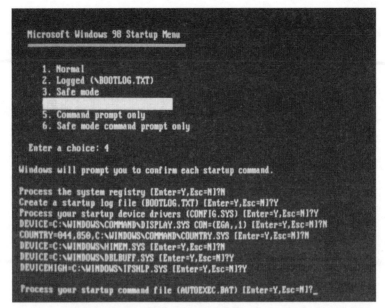

Fig.2.11 Step-by-step mode give good control over which boot processes are carried out

Try booting again but with the suspect process bypassed to see if this gets the PC booted into Windows. If that fails, try eliminating the process that occurs one stage earlier, then the one a further stage earlier, and so on. With luck you will soon get the system to boot, and the problem stage will be identified.

Error message

The cause of Windows stalling during start up is something you will not necessarily have to strive to discover. More often than not Windows will halt with a message stating the reason for everything suddenly grinding to a halt. Sometimes the problem will be due to a missing file. In fact in most instances it seems to be due to a damaged or missing file. A damaged file could be one that has become corrupted, but more usually it is one that has been overwritten by an earlier version of the same file. This is something we will consider in detail later in this chapter.

If the problem occurs after a piece of software has just been uninstalled, it is likely that the uninstaller removed a file that is needed by another program. The easy solution is to boot in Safe mode and reinstall the software, which should reinstate the file that Windows considers to be essential. Assuming that this is successful, you can either take the easy option and leave the reinstalled program in place, or try removing it again. The fact that the original removal of the program did not go entirely according to plan does not necessarily mean that a second attempt will also fail. On the other hand, it will not be a great surprise if it does fail.

It is worth making the point that installing and uninstalling software tends to be less troublesome if you always opt for the default directory rather than choosing another directory. I am not entirely sure why this should be, but it is probably due to minor errors in some installer and uninstaller programs. Anyway, unless there is a good reason to do otherwise, always settle for the default directory.

In the event of the boot process failing again, reinstalling the software once more should restore normal operation. You are not necessarily stuck with the program for life, and normal operation should be possible if the program is removed again and the contentious file is reinstated. The file causing the problem could be in the program's directory structure or in the Windows directory structure. Either way, using the file search function of Windows Explorer should soon locate it. Copy the file to a temporary directory and then uninstall the program. If the file was copied from somewhere in the Windows directory structure, copy it back to that location. If it was in the program's own directory structure, the directory it came from might have been removed by the uninstaller.

One approach to the problem is to remake part of the erased directory structure so that the file can be copied back to its original location. This might not be necessary though, and in most cases Windows will find the file if it is placed in the Windows directory structure where files of a similar type are located. In the case of a DLL file for example, Windows should find the file if it is copied to the Windows/System folder.

File hunt

In cases where reinstalling a recently uninstalled program is ineffective, or there is no recently uninstalled software to put back, reinstalling Windows is probably the best option. If Windows is reinstalled on top of the existing installation there should be no problems with your applications software. Any programs that are correctly installed with Windows should remain so after Windows itself has been reinstalled.

Although one might think that reinstalling Windows would always cure any boot problems, it is only fair to point out that it is not a universal panacea. In a fair proportion of cases it will get things back into working order, but sometimes the problem with the old installation is carried through into the new one. When Windows is installed over an existing installation, some of the settings from the old installation are copied to the new one. This provides a route for an existing problem to find its way into the new installation.

If no easy solution can be found to a Windows boot problem it is certainly worthwhile trying reinstallation before spending large amounts of time trying to precisely identify and cure the problem. Reinstalling Windows does not take all that long and there is a reasonable chance that it will get the operating system fully operational again. If the problem is due to a missing file, and it is a standard Windows file that has gone "absent without leave", reinstallation should get Windows running properly again. Similarly, if a standard Windows file has become corrupted, reinstalling Windows should overwrite the damaged file with a sound version and cure the problem. Installing Windows "from scratch" and on top of an existing installation are both covered in chapter 5.

Problems with missing and corrupted files often involve dynamic link library files, or DLL files as they are usually termed. These files are easily spotted when browsing the hard disc as they all have a "dll" extension. Some users make a backup copy of all the DLL files on the hard disc so that any files of this type that are accidentally erased or overwritten by an earlier version can be easily replaced. Backing up DLL files is covered in chapter 4. There will be a vast number of DLL files on the backup disc or directory, but if the one you require is actually there it should not take too long to locate it using the Find Folders or Files facility in Windows Explorer. It can then be copied to the appropriate folder using Windows Explorer.

Searching Windows

On the face of it, if a DLL file is damaged or missing and you think it might be on the Windows installation disc, browsing the disc should bring it to light. In practice there is a minor complication in that most of the Windows files are not stored on the installation disc as individual files. Instead you will find a number of cabinet files on the disc, and these are the ones that have a "cab" extension. Many of the Windows

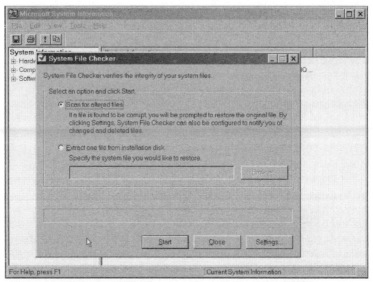

Fig.2.12 Running the System File Checker, which is part of the System Information program

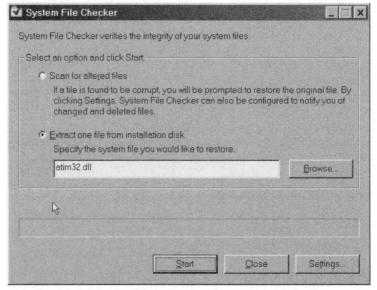

Fig.2.13 Selecting a file to be copied from the installation disc

files are compressed and grouped together in these cabinet files, but if you double-click on one of them using Windows Explorer, provided you are using Windows Me the files within each one will be shown as if they were separate entities. Furthermore, the files within a cabinet file can be copied using the normal Windows Explorer methods such as Copy and Paste.

This does not seem to work with Windows 95 or 98, but a decompression utility such as Winzip will show the contents of a cabinet file and permit the contents to be extracted. The MS/DOS Extract program should also do the job, but is relatively awkward to use. It can be found in the Windows\Command folder. In Windows 98 the System File Checker program can also be used to extract a file from the installation disc. This can be problematic in the first version of Windows 98, incidentally. It is probably worth trying if you use Windows 98 SE, but otherwise Winzip is a better bet.

In order to run the System File Checker program select Accessories from the Start menu and then choose System Information. Go to the Tools menu in the window that appears and select System File Checker.

This will produce a Window like the one in Figure 2.12. Activate the lower of the two radio buttons and type the name of the file you wish to extract from the Windows installation disc (Figure 2.13). Next operate the Start button, and type the source for the file and

Fig.2.14 Specifying the source and destination for the file

the location to which it is to be copied (Figure 2.14). Operate the OK button and the file should be extracted from the disc and copied to the specified destination directory.

Me safe

Using Windows Me it is possible to do your own troubleshooting when boot problems occur, but there is a troubleshooter Wizard to help sort out this type of problem. If you enter Safe mode using Windows Me you are greeted with a screen of the type shown in Figure 2.15. This gives

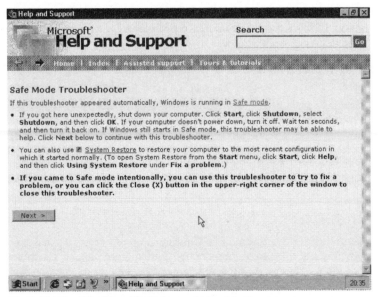

Fig.2.15 The Windows Me Safe mode troubleshooter

the option of using the System Restore program to take the system back to an earlier stage where it worked properly. System Restore is covered in chapter 4 and will not be considered in detail here. It is not applicable if the operating system has only just been installed, or there are problems installing it at all. It is not likely to help if the problem occurred after adding a new piece of hardware, or if an existing item of hardware is proving troublesome, but in most other cases it offers the quickest and easiest means of getting the computer operational again.

Operate the Next button if you decide to use the troubleshooter to sort things out. This produces the screen of Figure 2.16. The five radio buttons at the side of the window are used to select the description that best suits the way in which you ended up in Safe mode. These are the five descriptions:

I added new hardware and my computer started in Safe mode

During or immediately following Windows Millennium Setup my computer unexpectedly started in Safe mode

I added new software and my computer started in Safe mode

I don't know how I got here

Another troubleshooter instructed me to start in Safe mode

There is an omission here in that there is no option if you uninstalled some software and then had to start in Safe mode. Presumably either the third or fourth option should be used if this happens. In this example the PC had been working normally but for no apparent reason stopped in the middle

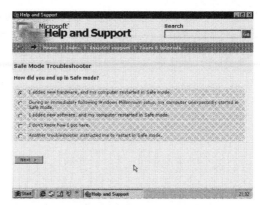

Fig.2.16 Starting to use the Windows Me troubleshooter

of the boot sequence with an error message. This gave the option of pressing Enter to return to Windows, but this failed to work. Probably because Windows had not finished booting and there was no Windows to boot into. The Control-Alt-Delete keys therefore had to be used to reboot the computer, which was then rebooted in Safe mode. Although not strictly accurate, the "I don't know" option seems the most appropriate.

Selecting this option and operating the Next button brings up the screen of Figure 2.17. This instructs the user to restart the computer. On restarting the computer it booted into Windows in Normal mode without any problems, and another reboot produced the same result. It was therefore unnecessary to go any further with the faultfinding process. As pointed out previously, a one-off start-up problem of this type is not unknown with

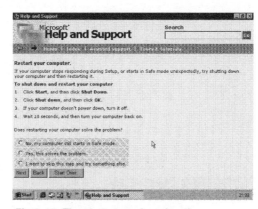

Fig.2.17 The next stage in using the Windows Me troubleshooter

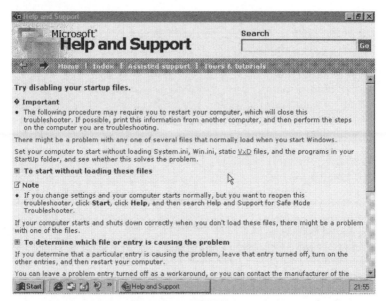

Fig.2.18 This help screen enables the PC to be booted into Windows without the Win.ini and System.ini files being processed

Windows, and it could be due to a glitch in Windows itself. It can also be caused by something like a piece of hardware not initialising properly when the computer is switched on. If a problem of this type only happens very infrequently it is probably not worth investigating further. With a very intermittent boot problem the chances of finding the cause are very limited.

If restarting the computer fails to clear the problem there is plenty of help available if the Safe mode is used again. For example, the screen of Figure 2.18 helps the user to try booting the computer without the Win.ini and System.ini files being processed. The screen of Figure 2.19 helps the user to restore an earlier version of the Windows Registry, and there are help screens for the usual steps when Windows troubleshooting.

Windows Registry

The Windows Registry seems to be regarded by many as the place to go in order to cure any Windows problem, but matters are not as simple as that. Problems with Windows are not necessarily due to anything

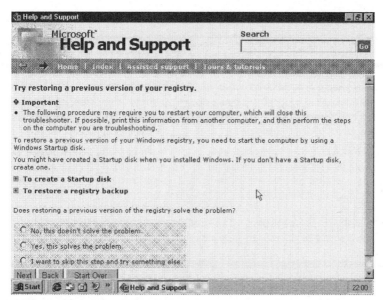

*Fig.2.19 This help screen enables an earlier version of the Windows
Registry to be restored*

amiss in the Registry. If a hardware driver is not installed properly or is
faulty, the Windows Registry is unlikely to provide an answer to the
problem. Perhaps of greater importance, even where editing the Registry
can clear a problem, unless great care is taken it is likely that the problem
will be made worse rather than better. Making any changes to the registry
has to be regarded as a high-risk activity.

As pointed out in chapter 1, Windows automatically produces backup
copies of the Registry, and it is possible to resort to one of these if the
Registry becomes seriously damaged. Also, you can make your own
backup copies of the Registry files, which can be restored if you somehow
manage to get the Registry files beyond redemption.

If you are determined to go ahead and experiment with editing the
Registry I would certainly recommend making backup copies just in
case things go seriously awry. Even if the Registry is well and truly
backed up, it is still not a good idea to start making changes unless you
are sure you know what you are doing. You can resort to a backup copy
if things go seriously awry, but realistically, your chances of success are
minimal.

What is it?

Probably most Windows users have heard of the Registry, but there are probably relatively few that know its exact nature and purpose. Although the name suggests that it is one file, it is actually two hidden files in the Windows folder called System.dat and User.dat. It is a database that contains all manner of Windows system settings. If you change settings via the Control Panel, you are actually making changes to the Windows Registry.

The same is true when you install or remove software or hardware, or make practically any changes to the system. It is not just the Windows settings that are stored in the Registry, and it can be used to store configuration information for applications programs as well. This factor probably increases the risk of the Registry being corrupted when software is installed or uninstalled. The Registry files can easily be damaged if the installer or uninstaller gets it slightly wrong.

Windows experts often edit the Registry as a means of customising their Windows installation. Obviously many aspects of Windows are easily changed via the standard routes, such as using the Control Panel to change things such as screen colours, resolution, etc. Hackers often prefer to go direct to the Registry because they can make some changes that are not possible via the approved channels. This is fine for those having the necessary expertise to make this type of change, but it is not to be recommended for occasional dabblers.

Editing

Many computer configuration files can be edited by simply loading them into a text editor or word processor and making the required changes.

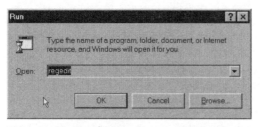

Fig.2.20 The Run option from the Start menu is used to run the Regedit program

This method is not normally used with the Registry files, and instead they are edited via the special editing utility. This program is called Regedit, and it can be found in the Windows directory. One way to run Regedit is to go to

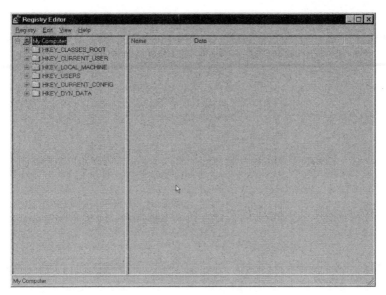

Fig.2.21 The initial screen of the Registry Editor

the Start menu, choose Run, type "regedit" in the text box, and then operate the OK button (Figure 2.20). There is no need to include the path to the Regedit.exe file; Windows will know where to find it. Alternatively, use the Run function but use the Browse facility to locate the Regedit.exe file and then operate the OK button. This will bring up the rather blank looking initial screen of Figure 2.21.

In operation Regedit is designed to be much like Windows Explorer. There are what appear to be files and folders, and there is no hint that it is actually two files that are being edited. You need to bear in mind the program is showing the contents of a database, and that it can not be used in exactly the same way as Windows Explorer. For example, the drag and drop approach does not work when using Regedit. Double clicking on one of the entries in the left-hand section of the screen expands it, as in Figure 2.22, to show what appear to be subfolders.

In Windows Registry terminology the left-hand section of the screen shows keys, and double clicking on one of these expands its entry to show the sub-keys. With subfolders double clicking on an entry will sometimes reveal further subfolders. Likewise, double clicking on sub-keys will sometimes reveal a further layer of the key structure. A mark beside a key icon indicates that a further layer of sub-keys is available.

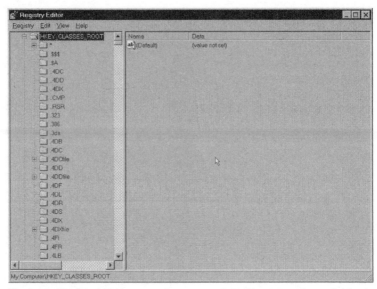

Fig.2.22 Double-clicking on a key expands it, like expanding a folder in Windows Explorer

Once the lowest level in the key structure has been reached, double clicking on an entry produces something like the window of Figure 2.23. Including the icons on the left, the right-hand section of the screen breaks down into three sections. The icon indicates the type of data stored in the key. An icon containing "ab" indicates that the key holds a string, which means that it contains letters and (or) numbers. The string is always contained within double quotation marks("). An icon containing "011110" indicates that the key holds a numerical code, which is often in the form of a binary number and not an ordinary decimal type. The hexadecimal numbering system is also used, and numbers of this type are preceded by "Ox" to show that they are in this numbering system. No quotation marks are used for numeric values.

Next to the icons in the Name column are the values, but this term is perhaps a bit misleading. The Name heading at the top of this column is more accurate, since the values are names that tell you which piece of data is stored for each entry in the database. Fortunately, the names used here usually give a good idea as to the purpose of each piece of data, although the names have to be kept reasonably short. The fourth column is the actual data stored in each value.

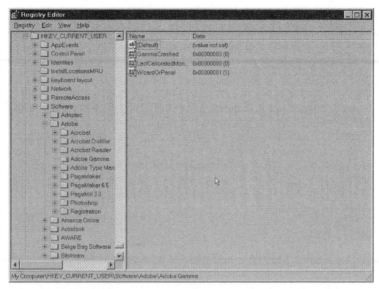

*Fig.2.23 Including the icons, the right-hand section of the screen
breaks down into three sections*

Navigation

You do not have to move around the Registry for long in order to realise
that the number of values stored there is vast. I do not know how many
values are to be found in an average Windows Registry, but it must be
many thousands. There are six main Registry keys in the "root directory",
which are known as "hive" keys incidentally. It is obviously much easier
to find the required value if you understand the significance of the hive
keys, and know which one to search. These are the six hive keys and
the types of value that each one contains:

HKEY_CLASSES_ROOT

All the file associations are stored within this key. This includes OLE
information, shortcut data, and file associations for the recognised file
types.

INKEY_CURRENT_USER

The desktop preferences are stored in this key. This mainly means
parameters that are set via the Control Panel, but other data is stored

here. Under the Software sub-key there is a further sub-key for each item of installed software, so there can be a vast number or entries here as well.

HKEY_LOCAL_MACHINE

Machine in a Windows context means the PC that it is running on. This hive key therefore contains data that is specific to the particular PC concerned. As one would expect, there is a Hardware sub-key here, but there are others such as a Network sub-key and a security type. There is a Software sub-key here as well, but it is different to the one found under the HKEY_CURRENT_USER hive key. The information stored in this Software sub-key seems to be largely associated with hardware configuration and uninstalling the software, rather than things like screen colours.

HKEY_USERS

If the PC has more than one user, this hive key is used to store the preferences for each user. In most cases the users feature of Windows is not utilized, so the information here will simply duplicate that stored in the HKEY_CURRENT_USER hive key. Perhaps more accurately, HKEY_CURRENT USERS will duplicate the data stored in HKEY_USERS.

HKEY_CURRENT_CONFIG

This key contains the current software and hardware configuration data. In the likely event that you are only using one configuration, it will contain the same data as HKEY_LOCAL_MACHINE.

HKEY_DYN_DATA

The dynamic data is stored in this hive key. Dynamic in this context means that it is data that must always be stored in memory so that it can be accessed quickly. As one would expect, the data stored here is highly technical in nature.

Even if you know what you are looking for and roughly where to find it, searching through the numerous entries in the Registry can still be very time consuming. Fortunately, the Registry Editor has a Find facility that is similar to the Find Files and Folders facility of Windows Explorer. Selecting Find from the Edit menu brings up a window like the one of Figure 2.24. Use the textbox to enter the text you wish to search for, and select the fields of the Registry you wish to search. You can also opt for a whole string search. In other words, a match will only be produced if the full string in the Registry matches the one you have entered.

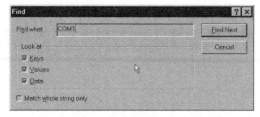

Fig.2.24 The Registry Editor's Find facility

If this option is not selected, a match will be produced if the string you entered matches part of an entry in the Registry. The whole string option can help to keep the number of matches to more manageable proportions, but you have to know precisely what you are looking for.

Press the Find Next button to search for the string. If a match is found, it will be shown highlighted in the main window of the Registry Editor. If this one is not the entry you are looking for, call up the Find facility again and operate the Find Next button. Keep doing this until the required entry is located or the whole of the Registry has been searched.

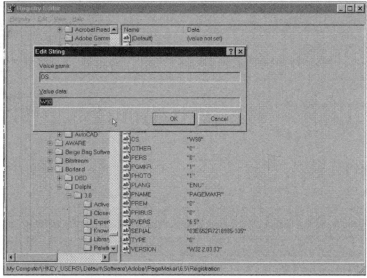

Fig.2.25 Editing an entry in the Registry

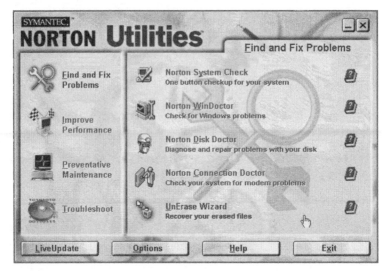

Fig.2.26 The opening screen of the Norton Utilities

In order to edit a Registry entry double-click on it to bring up the editing window, as in Figure 2.25. Both the value name and data can then be edited in the normal way. Left-click the OK button when you have finished, or the Cancel button if you change your mind. It is also possible to left-click on an entry and then use the Edit menu to either delete or rename it. Clearly it is necessary to know exactly what you are doing before altering any registry entries. If you suspect an entry is giving problems it is not possible to remedy the problem by editing its data unless you know the correct data to use. Unless you have the necessary expertise it is better to alter the Registry only via indirect routes, such as installing or uninstalling software, using the Control Panel, etc.

Backup

For inexperienced users it is better to rely on backup copies of the registry rather than fiddling with Registry settings when something goes wrong. Chapter 4 deals with the general topic of backups, including backing up and restoring the Registry. Windows runs the built-in Registry Checker program each time Windows is started, and it can also be run manually. From the Start menu select Programs, Accessories, System Tools, and System Information. Then select Registry Checker from the Tools menu of the window that appears.

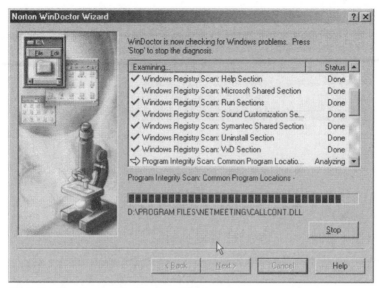

Fig.2.27 The Norton WinDoctor utility in action

If all is well, once the check has been completed you will be asked whether or not you wish to backup the Registry. It is automatically backed up each time Windows boots, so there is not usually any point in doing so. However, it will not do any harm to have a new backup produced. If Registry Checker finds a problem, which it never has in my experience, it will provide a warning message. Since Registry Checker runs automatically at start up, it will only find the newest of problems, which is presumably why it hardly ever finds anything wrong when run manually.

Windows checkers

There is not exactly a world shortage of software to help fix Windows problems. The software on offer ranges from simple utilities that are designed to investigate and fix problems in one particular aspect of Windows, to large suites of software that cover just about everything. These larger software suites often have utilities that are designed to "tune" the system and maintain it in peak condition. The Norton Utilities suite is probably the best known program of this type, and Figure 2.26 shows the start up screen. Here it is possible to select from a range of options, which include hard disc utilities, an enhanced Registry editor, and various

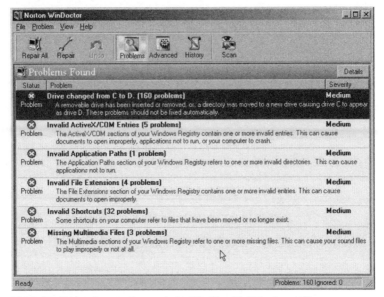

Fig.2.28 Example results produced by the DiskDoctor utility

diagnostic tools. Figure 2.27 shows the Norton WinDoctor facility in action, and amongst other things this scans the Windows Registry and other configuration files in search of errors.

Figure 2.28 shows an example of the test results produced by the WinDoctor utility. You always have to be slightly wary with this type of thing, because the checking utility might think it has found an error when things are in fact correct. The section of the report headed "Drive Changed from C to D" notes some 160 problems, but the PC in question is a dual boot type, and this has confused the checking utility. The problems that the program thinks it has found disappear when the PC is booted using the second hard disc drive. The program correctly advises against fixing the problems automatically. In most cases problems will be reported correctly, especially if your PC does not have an unusual configuration. Many of the faults can be fixed automatically by a program such as the Norton Utilities.

Sysedit

Sometimes Windows boot problems result in the system simply grinding to a halt, giving little clue as to what is wrong. Often though, Windows will provide an error message, and this is likely to refer to some form of Windows driver or system file that is mentioned in a configuration file. The problem can be due to the driver or other system file being absent or faulty, or it can simply be that the file is being called up in error. Uninstallers sometimes get things slightly wrong, and leave a reference to something like a driver or DLL file in a configuration file, even though that file is no longer needed and has been deleted. This might bring Windows to a halt during the boot-up process, but often the process can be continued without the missing file.

Normally when Windows reports that a file is missing it is necessary to reinstate it somehow. If a program has just been uninstalled, reinstalling the program will probably put the missing file back again. If the file in question is a standard Windows type that is present on the installation disc, it can be copied from the disc. Where the system seems to work perfectly well without the file, it is likely that the reference to it in the configuration file is erroneous.

You can simply put up with an error message being produced each time Windows boots, but it is better to remove the incorrect entry in the configuration file. The error message will usually mention the configuration file by name so that you know which one to edit. These files are usually straightforward text files, so they can be edited using a word processor or text editor. Whenever anything of this type is undertaken it is a good idea to make a copy of the file before you start editing. That way you can restore the backup copy if the changes make things worse rather than better.

Windows 95/98 has a built-in editor for the configuration files. It is called Sysedit, and it can be run by selecting Run from the Start menu, typing "sysedit" into the text box, and then operating the OK button. There is no need to give the path to the Sysedit program file. Running this program produces a window like Figure 2.29, with five windows open within the main window. Each of the five windows contains the text for a different configuration file. Two of these are for the MS/DOS configuration files autoexec.bat and config.sys.

The autoexec.bat file is used to run any ordinary programs that must be launched at the end of the boot process. Any programs mentioned in this file should be normal MS/DOS commands or program files. config.sys is similar, but it is used to run programs that have a sys extension. These are programs that can only be run from Config.sys, and they are mainly used to provide a background task such as a mouse driver.

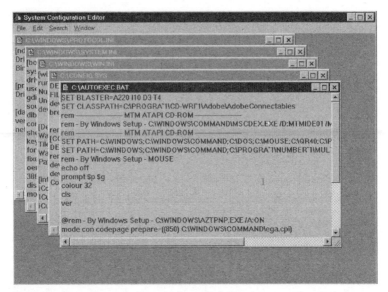

*Fig.2.29 Sysedit opens five configuration files in separate windows.
It is basically just a simple text processor*

The other three files are Windows configuration files, and in my
experience it is System.ini that is most likely to require editing. It is not
exactly unknown for Win.ini to require some adjustment, but I have never
yet needed to edit Protocol.ini. Both System.ini and Windows.ini have
their origins in the pre Windows 95 era, and are presumably retained
mainly to provide compatibility with software written for earlier versions
of Windows. The Windows Registry is the main source of configuration
data for Windows 95/98/Me. This does not mean that these two files are
no longer used by the system though, and mistakes in the initialisation
files can still cause problems with modern versions of Windows.

If you wish to edit a configuration file using Sysedit, left-click on its Window
to make it the current one, and it is a good idea to maximise the Window
as well. The text can then be edited in standard Windows word processor
or text editor fashion, and the usual facilities are available from the File
and Edit menus (Figure 2.30). These can be used to save the edited
version, but make sure that you save an unedited version under a different
name before you start making changes. If things go seriously wrong it
is then quite easy to return to the original version of the file.

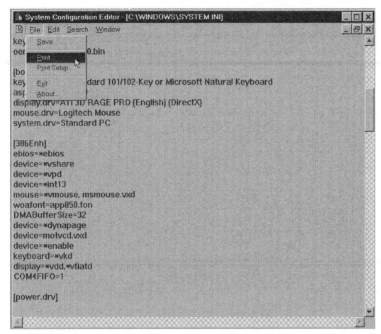

Fig.2.30 Sysedit has the usual File and Edit facilities

Reinstallation

If the usual methods of fixing Windows fail to get results, realistically there are only two options available. One is to continue searching for the cause of the problem, running diagnostic software, checking through configuration files, checking the hardware and drivers, or anything else you can think of. Option two is to reinstall Windows. Initially reinstall it on top of the existing version, which will leave your applications software properly installed and with luck will cure the problem. If that fails, any important data must be backed up to another hard disc or other mass storage device. The hard disc can then be wiped clean and Windows plus all the applications software and data must be reinstalled "from scratch".

This may seem like a defeatist attitude, but searching for the cause of an obscure fault in Windows can be very time consuming. A straightforward reinstallation is almost certain to be quicker, and even reinstalling Windows "from scratch" could be a quicker route to success. It is also

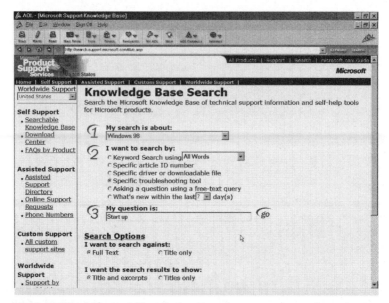

Fig.2.31 The Microsoft Knowledge Base has a good search engine

worth bearing in mind that reinstalling everything has the beneficial effect of removing the numerous unnecessary files that tend to start cluttering the hard disc as a Windows installation grows older. This will often produce a significant reduction in the time it takes for the system to boot, for programs to load and the general speed of operation when hard disc accesses are involved.

Where there is no easy solution to a Windows problem, professional PC maintenance engineers tend to opt for the reinstallation option sooner rather than later. For those with less experience of these things it will probably be more of a last resort than a routine method of fixing and streamlining a damaged Windows installation. However, having reinstalled everything you will probably be quite happy that you did.

Knowledge Base

In some circumstances there may be no option but to press on in an attempt to find a cure for the problem. With masses of important data on the hard disc and no means of backing it up, wiping the disc clean is

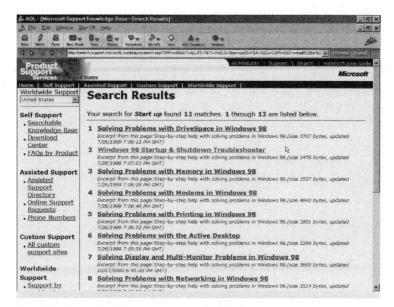

*Fig.2.32 The search engine succeeded in finding a start up
             troubleshooter*

not an option. The best course of action would be to have the computer
fitted with some form of mass storage device so that the data could be
backed up. Apart from leaving your reinstallation options open, this
also guards against losing important data due to a hard disc failure. If
you have an Internet connection and decide to press on rather than
reinstall, it is worthwhile investigating the Microsoft Knowledge Base.
There is actually a massive amount of help available at Microsoft's web
site (www.microsoft.com), including articles and troubleshooting Wizards
for a large range of Microsoft products.

A good place to start is the Self Support section. This brings up a screen
like the one in Figure 2.31, where you can specify the product for which
you require support, and the type of support required (article,
troubleshooter, driver file, etc.). You can also put in some key words to
help the search engine come up with something suitable. If Windows
will not start up properly for example, "start up problem" will help the
search engine to come up with some suitable suggestions.

A search for a Windows 98 troubleshooter to assist with a start up problem
produced the screen of Figure 2.32. Here there is a troubleshooter for

problems with both starting up and closing down Windows. This asks the user questions and then makes suggestions on how to fix the problem. With perseverance, I would guess that practically any Windows problem could be solved using the information available from the Microsoft Knowledge Base. The only problem is that you will probably need a second PC to access the Internet while your faulty PC is being sorted out. Possibly a friend can assist if you do not have a spare computer.

Recurring problems

If you are very unlucky, having reinstalled everything "from scratch" the problem will return again. It is likely that the problem will keep reappearing if you keep reinstalling Windows. Where the problem is in some way hardware related, perhaps only happening when the soundcard is used, the most likely explanation is that one of the drivers or the hardware itself is faulty. It is more likely to be a driver problem than a fault in the hardware, so check with the technical support department of the hardware manufacturer to see if a later version of the driver software is available. These days most manufacturers have the latest drivers available on their web sites, where there may also be some troubleshooting hints, so the relevant web site should be the first port of call.

If everything works fine at first, but things go seriously wrong after a while or steadily worsen, the most likely culprit is an applications program. Finding the program that is causing the problem can be quite time consuming. If one program consistently goes "walkabout" and all the others work perfectly, it is virtually certain that the troublesome program is responsible for its own downfall. It is possible for one program to interfere with the system and cause problems with just one other program, but this is quite rare. Normally this occurs because installing one program results in a DLL file for a second program being overwritten with an older version of the file. Provided the problem is fixed by reinstating the newer version of the file there should be no further difficulties. If you simply keep reinstalling Windows and then install the applications in the same order, the problem will keep coming back. Installing the applications in reverse order should banish the problem, since the newer version of the DLL file will then replace the older version, rather than the other way round.

It is more common for the faulty software to damage the Windows installation, causing problems for itself and for other applications programs. The normal solution where recurring problems occur is to reinstall Windows plus one application. If that works all right for a while add a further application. If all is well add another application, and so on until a program is added and things start to go awry. It is then a reasonable assumption that the last program to be added is the one that is damaging the Windows installation.

Points to remember

If Windows fails to boot properly, do not be too eager to start fiddling with the system to find a cure. Try rebooting a few times to see if the problem clears itself.

Where the boot process halts quite early it is likely that the problem is in booting MS/DOS. Check the Autoexec.bat and Config.sys files for repetitive entries and other obvious errors, such as hardware drivers that are not needed any more.

Unless the Windows installation is badly damaged it will be possible to boot in Safe mode. Some basic checks can then be made, such as running Scandisk, etc., but bear in mind that Safe mode has some limitations.

Getting the computer to produce a Bootlog file can help to pinpoint the process that is causing the boot process to stall.

Booting in step-by-step mode can also be used to find the stage that is causing problems. By bypassing sections of the boot process a process of elimination can be used to find the one that is causing the problem.

Device Manager can be used to check whether or not the hardware and the hardware drivers are functioning correctly, but not with the computer booted in Safe mode. Get the computer booted in normal mode, even if this means bypassing some boot processes so that Windows is something less than fully operational.

If a hardware driver is suspected of causing problems, use Device Manager to remove the existing driver before reinstallation. Also check the hardware manufacturer's web site for an up-dated driver.

Windows will often give an error message that gives some clue to the nature of the problem. If a program has recently been uninstalled, reinstalling it will probably reinstate the damaged or missing file.

Installing a program can also damage a file. This can result in a file being overwritten by an older version. Reinstalling Windows or one of the other application files will cure this problem. If the damaged file is on the Windows installation disc it can be copied from the disc using a file decompression program (Winzip, etc.).

In some cases the missing file is not actually needed any more. Removing the reference to it in a configuration file will then cure the problem.

Windows includes a Registry Editor program, but only use this utility if you know what you are doing.

Reinstalling Windows over the existing installation will cure boot problems in a fair proportion of cases, but not all of them.

Reinstalling Windows from scratch will cure boot problems unless it is not really a Windows problem. Recurring problems are due to a hardware fault or a bug in an applications program.

There are numerous Windows checking programs available, and these will often help to sort out boot problems, and more minor annoyances. Many will also help to keep Windows working efficiently.

Windows Me has a troubleshooter that provides a great deal of help if the PC is booted in Safe mode. You can still do your own investigations if you prefer.

Similar help for other versions of Windows can be found at the Microsoft web site (www.microsoft.com).

Windows Me has a very useful restore facility that will usually cure boot problems. There are Registry backup facilities and other facilities in Windows 95/98 that can often be effective. These topics are covered in detail in chapter 4.

Data rescue

Learning the hard way

A hard disc failure is potentially a major disaster for all those who use the PC, but if you use PCs for some years it is a failure you are almost certain to experience. A complete failure of the disc means that all the data it contains is lost. There are companies that offer a data recovery service, but there is no guarantee that the contents of the disc will be recoverable, and the cost of a recovery service is too high for many users anyway. As a minimum, any important data files should be backed up onto floppy discs, CDRs, or any suitable media, so that they can be restored onto a new hard disc if the old unit fails.

Ideally the entire contents of the hard disc drive should be backed up using a program that enables it to be properly restored onto a new hard disc. This is very much quicker and easier than having to reinstall and configure the operating system, and then reinstall all the applications programs and data. Also, any customisation of the operating system or other software will be automatically restored. If you have heavily customised software, after reinstallation it can take a great deal time to get it set up to your satisfaction.

Having a backup copy of the hard disc's contents is not only insurance against a loss of valuable data if a hardware failure occurs. It can greatly simplify things if there is a major problem with the operating system. Provided the PC was fully operational when the backup copy was made, resorting to the backup will provide a fully functioning PC again. Some backup software enables the system to be quickly restored to a previous and fully working configuration, but retains any recently produced data files. The Windows Me Restore utility provides a facility of this type, but it is not present in earlier versions of Windows. When a major problem with the operating system occurs and some form of restoration option is available, it is almost certainly best to resort to this method sooner rather than later.

There is little point in spending large amounts of time trying to repair a damaged installation if it can be replaced with a backup copy quite quickly and easily. It is certainly worthwhile spending a small amount of time first to check for any minor problems that are easily sorted out. The backup method is "using a sledgehammer to crack a nut" if the problem is something minor that is easily corrected. If a search for any obvious problems proves to be in vain, it is time to resort to the backup software. The backup program's manual should give detailed instructions on maintaining an up-to-date backup and restoring the hard disc's contents.

The problem with the full back up method is that it takes a fair amount of time to maintain an up to date copy of the hard disc. Also, it is only feasible if your PC is equipped with some form of mass storage device that can be used for backup purposes, such as a CDR writer or a Zip drive. It could otherwise require well in excess of a thousand floppy discs to do a full backup of the hard drive! Even using some form of mass storage it can take a long while to backup the gigabytes of programs and data stored on many modern hard disc drives. The quickest and easiest way of providing a backup is to opt for a second hard disc drive. Due to the current low cost of hard discs, this could well be the cheapest method as well.

Split discs

Many PC users now split their large hard drives into two logical drives, which become drives C: and D: as far as the operating system is concerned. Drive C: is then used in the normal way and drive D: is reserved for backup purposes. This method is useless in the event that the hard drive develops a serious fault, because the main and backup drives are the two halves of one physical drive. If one becomes faulty it is unlikely that the other will be usable either. The point of this system is that the backup copy on drive D: is usable if there is a software problem rather than a fault in the hardware. Since most users have far more problems with the software than with hard disc faults, this method should get the user out of trouble more often than not.

Some users take a compromise approach and make a backup copy of the hard disc when it contains a newly installed operating system having all the hardware properly integrated into the operating system and fully operational. Ideally the disc should also have the applications programs installed, and any customisation completed. Any important data is backed up separately as it is generated. If the operating system becomes seriously damaged it is then easy to resort to the backup which should be reasonably compact, but gives you a basic system that is fully customised and ready to use. Any essential data can also be restored, but there is no need to restore any data files that are no longer needed on the hard disc.

Clean copy

An advantage of this method is that it returns the PC to a "clean" copy of the operating system. Over a period of time most modern operating systems seem to become slightly "gummed up" with numerous files that no longer serve any purpose, and things can generally slow down. By returning to a fresh copy of the operating system you will probably free up some hard disc space and things might run slightly faster. By not restoring any unimportant data files you free up further hard disc space.

If you lack a proper backup copy of the hard disc and only have copies of the data files, all is not lost. In this situation you might prefer to put a fair amount of effort into fixing the damaged Windows installation rather than simply reinstalling everything. Even if you only use a few applications programs, reinstalling Windows and the applications software is likely to be pretty tedious and time consuming. If there are numerous programs to reinstall, the process is likely to be very tedious and time consuming.

Looking on the bright side, if everything does have to be restored from scratch you will have a "clean" copy of the operating system that should provide optimum performance. In fact many users habitually take the reinstallation route and consider any extra time and effort involved being well worthwhile.

I would not go as far as to advocate reinstalling everything at the first sign of trouble, but I would definitely advise against the opposite approach of always repairing the original set up regardless of how long it takes. Apart from the fact this could be a very time consuming approach, an installation that has been patched up on numerous occasions, and perhaps had a number of programs added, upgraded, and removed over a period of time, is unlikely to provide peak performance. In fact I have encountered several installations of this type that took an eternity to go through the boot-up sequence, in one case taking almost 10 minutes to complete the process! Once booted, PCs of this type seem to give the hard disc drive a "hammering" at every opportunity. Apart from making the computer slow and irksome in use, this type of thing increases the wear on the hard disc drive and presumably shortens its operating life. It should be possible to discover the sources of the problem and improve results, but reinstalling everything "from scratch" is the solution favoured by most when this situation arises. This should ensure optimum performance and might be quicker anyway.

Windows on Windows

On the face of it there is no need to wipe the hard disc clean and undertake a complete reinstallation from the beginning. Simply reinstalling Windows over the old installation should restore normality. As with so many things in computing it is a case of yes and no. Yes, in some cases simply going through the Windows set up routine will fix problems with the operating system and restore normal operation. Unfortunately, in other cases the problem will still exist once the reinstallation is complete. When Windows is installed on a hard disc, the Windows Setup program searches the disc for a previous installation and installed Windows application programs. Any installed software will be integrated with the new Windows installation, as may driver programs and other support files.

As a consequence, having reinstalled Windows it should not be necessary to reinstall the applications software as well. The down side is that any files giving problems with the old installation may be retained, in the new one. Having reinstalled the operating system you could well find that it does not work any better than before. My experiences suggest that reinstalling Windows on top of the existing installation probably has little more than a 50 percent chance of success. As it is a reasonably quick and easy process it is probably worthwhile giving it a try before resorting to an installation "from scratch", but do not be surprised if it does not have the desired effect.

Do not be tempted to try upgrading to a newer version of Windows by installing it on top of a non-working version. People sometimes try this, working on the basis that the new version will have little dependency on the old one, and the problem with the old version will be "blown away" by the new version. In practice there is little likelihood of this happening. The Windows Setup program may detect that there is a problem and refuse to go ahead with the upgrade. If it does proceed, the most likely outcome is that the reinstallation will go very wrong somewhere along the line, and that it will never be completed. If you do manage to get the new version installed, it will probably have more problems than the old one.

Preliminaries

If you do decide to go ahead with reinstallation "from scratch" it is essential to backup any important data files first. If you are using heavily customised applications programs it is also a good idea to make copies of the configuration files so that the customisation files are easily reinstated. In fact any files that are unique to your particular installation should be backed-up, including things like speech profiles of voice recognition programs. Some of your applications programs may have facilities for saving and reinstating customisation files. In other cases simply overwriting the default files with your customised versions will probably have the desired effect.

It is worth emphasising that backing-up important files should not be left until the PC gives problems. If there is a serious fault in the hard disc it may be impossible to recover any files that have not been backed-up. Matters are less dire if the problem lies in the operating system rather than the disc itself, but it could still be difficult to make backup copies of important files. With the computer not booting into the operating system properly, you are unlikely to have proper access to all the drives and applications programs. Provided Safe Mode is functioning properly you can boot into a version of Windows, but one where drives other than the hard and floppy discs will not be functioning. This limits your backup options. There are ways of making a backup of a hard disc drive in an emergency, but this might involve buying some additional hardware. It is better to avoid getting into situations where drastic measures are needed in order to recover the situation.

Floppy discs

Floppy discs are suitable for backup purposes where only a limited amount of data is involved. The upper limit depends on how many floppy discs you are prepared to use, a factor that is probably a reflection of how desperate you are! Backing up 30 megabytes of data onto about 20 or so floppy discs will be quite time consuming, but is still well within the bounds of reason. Backing up several hundred megabytes onto dozens of floppy discs is not a very practical proposition, and the discs could well cost more than some more convenient backup systems! In terms of megabytes per pound, floppy discs are not very competitive these days.

Where floppy discs are suitable, there is a potential problem in that some of the files you wish to copy may be too big to fit on a single floppy disc.

The capacity of a high-density 3.5-inch floppy disc is 1.44 megabytes when the standard PC disc format is used. Things like DTP and graphics files can be substantially larger than this. The normal copying facilities of MS/DOS and Windows can not spread a large file across one or more discs. If you try to copy a file that is too large to fit onto the disc an error message to that effect will be produced. Fortunately, there are several MS/DOS and Windows programs that can handle this problem. The later versions of the popular Winzip program for example, will compress and copy large files to several floppy discs if necessary. You can even copy a collection of files and save them as one large file spread across several discs.

Large scale

If floppy discs are not up to the task it is clearly necessary to resort to some form of mass storage device. It is highly unlikely that any installed device of this type will work in Safe Mode, including a simple read-only CD-ROM drive, but it might be possible to get non-standard drives to operate in MS/DOS. In this context, non-standard means just about anything other than a floppy disc drive or an IDE hard disc drive.

With Windows 95 and 98 you have the option of restarting the computer in MS/DOS mode. From the Start menu select Shut down and Restart in MS/DOS mode. The computer can also be started in MS/DOS mode pressing F8 as the computer starts to boot into Windows, and then selecting the appropriate option from the menu. Neither of these routes is available in Windows Me. The MS/DOS prompt is still available via the Start button and the Programs menu option, but this is unlikely to be of much help.

In fact you may find that the mass storage device mysteriously disappears from the operating system's repertoire when the PC is booted in MS/ DOS mode. In the case of a CD writer it may still be accessible, but only for reading purposes. Trying to write files to it will probably produce an error message. It is possible that the storage device simply lacks MS/ DOS compatibility, in which case it will only be usable if you can get Windows largely operational again. It is more likely that the device can be used with MS/DOS, but the MS/DOS drivers are not installed by default. The instruction manual for the drive should make it clear whether or not the device can be used with MS/DOS.

If it can, installation instructions and the necessary software should be included with the drive. Usually the easiest way of tackling the problem is to make a bootable floppy disc and to then boot the PC using this.

The simplest way of making a bootable disc is to place a blank (formatted or unformatted) floppy disc in drive A: and then issue this command at the MS/DOS prompt:

format A:/s

Follow any onscreen prompts, and the disc will then be formatted after which the system files will be copied onto it. This gives a basic boot disc, but the support software for the mass storage device must then be installed onto the disc. The drive's instruction manual should give detailed installation instructions, and may well give full details of how to make an emergency boot disc. Note that the BIOS settings may have to be changed before the PC will boot from a floppy disc. Changing drive and boot settings in the BIOS is covered later in this chapter.

Second disc

If you have large amounts of data to backup and no mass storage device, your choices are limited. One option is to simply keep trying to repair the Windows installation until you are successful. Any Windows installation should be repairable, and persistence should eventually pay off. You may get lucky and fix the problem fairly quickly, or a great deal of time could be involved in locating and removing the problem. The biggest drawback of this method is that you will still have no backup of the hard disc's contents, limiting your options if there are further problems with the Windows installation. Also, the contents of the disc will probably be lost forever if the drive becomes faulty.

Many users save data onto a hard disc thinking that their work is safe and secure, but this is definitely not the case. Having data on a hard disc is sometimes likened to hanging paper documents by a thin thread over an open fire. Modern hard drives are relatively reliable, but if used for long enough a hard disc drive will go wrong, and you will probably end up throwing away the drive together with all your hard work.

A better option is to add some form of mass storage device. An external (parallel port) Zip drive is not particularly expensive, and in an emergency it should work quite happily with the computer booted into MS/DOS. A few Zip discs can store several hundred megabytes of data, which should be sufficient to backup any important data files, configuration files, etc. Note that any form of USB or SCSI storage device is unlikely to work with Windows in Safe mode or with MS/DOS. This is simply because the interface will not be recognised in Safe mode or in MS/DOS, rendering the drive "invisible" to the operating system.

My preferred option is to add another hard disc drive. These days this probably represents the cheapest means of adding large amounts of extra storage capacity to a PC, and a hard disc also has the advantage of being very fast. Read and write speeds are measured in megabytes per second, unlike some other storage systems where it is specified as so many megabytes per minute. A further advantage of the hard disc approach is that the disc should work properly with Windows booted in Safe Mode, or with the PC booted in MS/DOS mode. It should even work using the Windows MS/DOS Prompt program. A hard disc drive is one of the standard PC drives, and as such it does not require any special drivers for basic operation. This makes life easier at the best of times, but greatly eases things when the Windows installation is damaged.

Adding a drive

Fitting a second hard disc drive obviously requires the lid or side panel of the PC to be removed, followed by some delving around inside the computer. It is not one of the more difficult upgrades, but unless you are reasonably practical it would be advisable to have the upgrade done professionally. Most shops that sell hard disc drives also offer an upgrade service, but it will almost certainly cost substantially more to have the drive fitted for you. However, this extra cost is preferable to damaging the PC and having to pay a hefty repair bill. Assuming that you feel confident enough to go ahead with the upgrade yourself, the first task is to open up the PC to determine the current configuration.

With older PCs the top and two sides of the case are in one piece, and are released by removing four or six screws at the rear of the unit. Be careful, because there will probably be other screws here that hold other things in place, such as the power supply unit. With the right screws removed the outer casing should pull away upwards and rearwards, but it will probably take a certain amount of force to pull it free. More modern cases have removable side panels, and in most cases these are again held in place by four or six screws at the rear of the unit. Both panels must be removed in order to give full access to the drive bays. If your PC has one of the more unusual case styles it will be necessary to carefully examine the exterior in order to "crack" it.

A modern PC has the hard disc interface on the motherboard rather than provided by an expansion card. In fact there are two hard disc interfaces on the motherboard, or possibly four on a modern PC. These are known as IDE interfaces, and this simply stands for integrated drive electronics. In other words, most of the electronics for the hard disc drive controller is built into the drive itself. At one time the IDE interfaces were strictly for hard disc drives, but in a modern PC they can be used for other types of drive. These multipurpose interfaces are more accurately called EIDE interfaces, which stands for enhanced integrated drive electronics. In practice they are still often referred to as just plain IDE interfaces. Many types of drive can be used with an EIDE interface, including CD-ROM, Zip, and LS120 drives.

In a typical PC the hard disc drive is connected to IDE port 1 and the CD-ROM drive is wired to IDE port 2. However, each IDE interface supports up to two devices, so the hard disc and CD-ROM drive could be connected to IDE port 1 via a single cable. Assuming that your PC has no more than three internal drives, excluding any floppy drives, it should certainly be able to support another hard drive. If you look at the cabling inside the PC you should find some wide cables, know as "ribbon" cables, that connect the drives to the motherboard. With luck, at least one of these cables will have an unused connector that can be used with the new drive.

Note that any spare connector on the drive that connects to the floppy disc drive is of no use with a hard disc drive. The floppy variety uses a completely different interface having a smaller connector. A suitable power supply lead and connector is also needed. The connectors come in two sizes, which are a larger one for 5.25-inch drives and a smaller one for the 3.5-inch variety (Figure 3.1). However, all the hard disc drives I have encountered use the larger connector regardless of whether they fit 3.5-inch or 5.25-inch bays.

Fig.3.1   3.5-inch (left) and 5.25-inch (right) power connectors

If you are out of luck, one or other of the required leads and connectors will not be present. If the hard disc and CD-ROM drive share an IDE interface, the other IDE interface will be available for the additional drive, but it will not be fitted with a cable. Another possibility is that the existing drives are connected to separate IDE interfaces using single cables rather than types having two connectors for drives. In either case a standard twin IDE data lead is needed in addition to the drive (Figure 3.2).

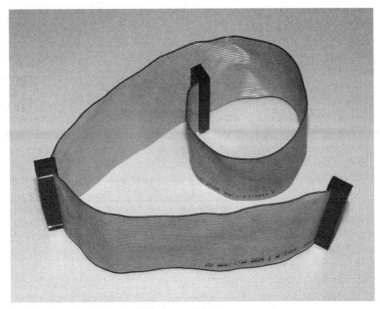

Fig.3.2 A standard twin IDE data cable

Bare facts

Hard drives are available in so called "bare" and "retail" or "boxed" versions. A bare drive may consist of nothing more than the drive itself. However, it will usually include an instruction manual and a set of fixing screws, but no data cable. Incidentally, if you find yourself with a hard drive but no matching manual, the web sites of most hard disc manufacturers include downloadable versions of the manuals for most of their hard disc units. Unless you are dealing with a very old or unusual drive, the information you require should be available on the manufacturer's web site.

The retail versions of hard drives normally include a cable in addition to a set of fixing screws and a more comprehensive manual. There may be other items such as a mounting cradle to permit a 3.5-inch drive to be used in a 5.25-inch drive bay. With modern drives there may well be two data cables included with the drive. One of these is a standard IDE cable that can be used with any IDE drive and any IDE interface. The other cable enables the drive to be used with a modern IDE interface that supports UDMA66 or possibly the new UDMA100 standard. UDMA66 and UDMA100 have the potential of faster data transfers than older standards such as the UDMA33 variety, but they can only be used if they are supported by the motherboard, the drive itself, and the correct cable is used.

The instruction manual for your PC should state whether or not it supports anything beyond UDMA33. If in doubt, the safe option is to use a standard IDE cable. This may provide something less than the ultimate in performance, but the disc should still work very well. It should certainly work well enough for making a backup of the main drive. Drive speeds are improving, but with many drives it is still the drive itself rather than the interface that limits performance. Do not try to use a mixture of UDMA33 and UDMA66 or UDMA100 devices on one interface. The cable will only be right for one type or the other, and each interface can only work in one mode or the other. It is perfecly all right to have UDMA33 devices on one IDE interface and UDMA66 or UDMA100 devices on the other.

Static

If you buy virtually any computer add-on to fit inside a PC it will be supplied in packaging plastered with dire warnings about the dangers of static electricity. Some of these are a bit "over the top", and suggest that going anywhere near the device without the protection of expensive anti-static equipment will result in it being instantly zapped. In reality the risks of static induced damage occurring are probably quite small. On the other hand, computer add-ons have yet to fall in price so far that they are in the "two a penny" category, and the risk of damage occurring is a real one. By observing a few simple rules the likelihood of damage can be reduced to insignificant proportions.

Rule number one is to leave the device in its packaging until it is time to install it. The plastic bags, foam lined boxes, etc., used for computer bits and pieces are designed to keep static electricity at bay. In some cases the packaging is designed to insulate the contents from high voltages. In others it is designed to conduct electricity so that no significant charge can build up between any two points in the device being protected. Any charges of this type will be almost instantly short-circuited by the conductive packaging.

Rule number two is to make sure that you are not charged with a high static voltage that could damage the device when you remove it from the packing. When working on computers do not wear clothes that are known to be good generators of static electricity. Manmade fibres are the most prolific static generators, but most modern clothes are made from natural fibres or a mixture of manmade and natural fibres, so this is not the major problem that it was at one time.

To make quite sure that both yourself and the device being installed are charge free, hold the device in its packing in one hand, and touch something that is earthed with the other hand. Any charge in you or the device should then leak away to earth. The metal case of the computer is a convenient earth point. With the cover or side panels removed there should be plenty of bare metal to touch. Touching the paintwork will not provide reliable earthing since most paints are excellent electrical insulators. Note that the computer must be plugged into the mains supply, but it does not have to be switched on.

Rule number three is to keep the work area free of any large static charges. Any obvious sources of static charges should be removed from the vicinity of the computer. Television sets and computer monitors are good static generators, which means that the computer must be moved away from the monitor before you start work on it. This will normally be necessary anyway, because with the computer's base unit in its normal location it will probably be difficult to get proper access to the interior of the unit. It needs to be placed on a table where there is good access to the interior and plenty of light so that you can see what you are doing.

The table should preferably be one that it not precious, but if necessary the top can be protected with something like a generous quantity of old newspapers. It is a good idea to have the PC plugged into the mains supply but switched off at the mains socket. The earthed metal chassis of the computer will then tend to earth any static charges in its vicinity, preventing any dangerous charges from building up.

If you follow these simple rules it is very unlikely that the add-on device will be damaged by static charges. When dealing with hard disc drives it is as well to bear in mind that they are relatively delicate physically. Modern drives, although more intricate, are not as vulnerable as the early types. Even so, dropping a hard disc drive onto the floor is definitely not a good idea!

Jumpers

An IDE device has configuration jumpers that are used to set whether the unit will be used as the master or slave device on its IDE channel. Even if there is only one device on an IDE channel, that device must still

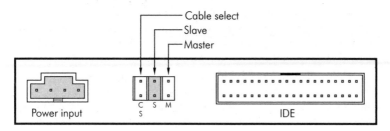

Fig.3.3 Typical layout for the rear of an IDE drive

be set as the master or slave unit. By convention, a single drive on an IDE channel is set as the master device. Therefore, if you are adding the new disc to an IDE channel that already has one device installed, the new drive must be set to operate as the slave device. If the new drive will be the sole device on its IDE channel, it must be set for master operation.

The rear of most CD-ROM drives and some IDE hard disc drives look something like Figure 3.3. The connector on the left is the power input and the one on the right is for

the data cable. In between these are three pairs of terminals that can be bridged electrically by a tiny metal and plastic gadget called a jumper. A jumper can be seen in place in Figure 3.4. The "cable select" option is not used in a PC context, so only two pairs of contacts are relevant here. You simply place the jumper on the master or slave contacts, depending on which option you require. The

Fig.3.4 A jumper fitted to a drive

configuration jumper should be supplied with the drive incidentally, and is normally set at the master option by default on a hard disc drive.

With hard disc drives matters are not always as simple as the arrangement shown in Figure 3.3. There is often an additional set of terminals, and these are used where the drive will be used as the only device on an IDE channel. Using this setting will allow a lone drive to be correctly identified and used by the PC. If the drive has these additional terminals (or they are fitted in place of the cable select pins), you must use them for a sole IDE drive, as it is unlikely that the drive will be picked up properly by the BIOS if the normal master setting is used. Getting it wrong is not likely to produce any damage, but the drive will be unusable until the mistake has been corrected. The manual supplied with the drive should give details of the configuration settings available.

If the new drive is used as the slave device on the primary IDE channel, the other hard drive will presumably be the master device on this channel. The existing drive will need its configuration setting altered if it is set to operate as the sole IDE device on its channel. The manual supplied with the PC should give details of the configuration settings. Alternatively, it should be possible to identify the drive from its markings, and it will almost certainly be possible to find its instruction manual on the Internet.

Where there is no device on the secondary IDE channel, or only a CD-ROM, it would probably be best to add the new drive on this channel. If a CD-ROM is present on this channel, adding the new drive as the secondary slave device is unlikely to require any configuration changes to the CD-ROM drive. If no device is already present, simply add the new drive as the master device or sole device, as appropriate. In theory, data exchanges between the two hard disc drives will be quicker if they are on different IDE channels, so where possible it is better to arrange things this way.

It is definitely a good idea to check the configuration setting of the new drive, and where necessary alter it, prior to fitting the drive in the case. Once the drive is fitted inside the case it can be difficult to get at the jumper and terminals, and it can be very difficult indeed to see what you are doing when adjusting the jumper.

Getting physical

It is not essential to install the new hard drive in the computer as a fixture. You may prefer to simply connect the new drive to the data and power cables, do the backup, reinstallation and restoration, and then disconnect the drive again. It can then be stored safely away somewhere in case it is needed at some later date. With the drive in storage rather than in use it should not wear out, and should be ready for use if it is needed a few years "down the line". I used this method successfully with a couple of PCs for many years, although not strictly out of choice.

With a PC that has one of the minimalist cases you may find that there are no spare bays for another hard disc drive. Note that it is possible to use a 3.5-inch drive in a 5.25-inch drive bay using an adapter. This is

Fig.3.5 The connections on the underside of the drive must not be allowed to come into contact with the chassis, etc.

just a metal cradle into which the drive is bolted, and the whole assembly then fits into the drive bay just like a 5.25-inch drive. This adapter should be available from any large computer store. As pointed out previously, it is sometimes (but not always) included with boxed retail versions of hard disc drives.

When temporarily connecting a drive it is essential to make sure that no exposed connections on the unit come into electrical contact with the metal case, expansion cards, etc. Some drives are fully enclosed, but most have the underside of the circuit board exposed (Figure 3.5). Often the easiest way of keeping the drive safe is to place it on top of the computer with some newspaper to insulate the drive from the case. With a PC that has some form of tower case it is usually easier to work on the unit if it is placed on its side. The drive can then be placed on the side of the drive cage, again with newspaper being used to provide insulation.

Probably most users will wish to use the additional disc as a permanent feature. This is essential if you wish to use it to make frequent backups or you will be making backup copies of data files as they are generated. If you are using a drive bay that has no front opening, the new drive must be slid in from the rear. Any expansion cards that get in the way must be removed temporarily. Remove the screws that fix the cards to the rear of the chassis and it should then be possible to pull the cards free.

The sockets on the drive are at the rear, so the other end is pushed into the rear of the drive bay. The manufacturer's name, etc., are marked on the top plate of the drive, so this side should be facing upward. In most cases the drive can be fully pushed into the bay, but it is sometimes necessary to ease it back slightly to get the mounting holes in the drive and the bay to match up properly.

In days gone by it was necessary to use plastic guide rails to mount the drives in the case, but any PC made within the last seven years or more should have drive bays that take the drives without the need for these rails. Four mounting bolts are normally supplied with the drive, and these are used to secure it to the bay. If no fixing screws were supplied with the drive, the PC may have been supplied with some odds and ends of hardware. If so, there will probably be some suitable screws in amongst these. Failing that, you will have to buy some metric M3 screws about 6 millimetres long. Note that the mounting screws must be quite short, and should not protrude more than a few millimetres into the drive. Longer mounting bolts could easily damage something inside the drive.

With a so-called "external" drive bay, it might be easier to insert the drive from the front. Where the interior of the computer is very crowded this can avoid having to remove expansion cards to get the drive in place. An external bay is really intended for use with a floppy drive, CD-ROM drive, or some other type where access is needed to the drive for changing discs. However, an external bay is perfectly suitable for a wholly internal drive such as a hard disc unit. The plastic cover at the very front of the bay can be carefully prised out using a flat bladed screwdriver, and it might then be possible to slide the drive in through the front of the case. There will probably be a metal plate behind the plastic cover though. It may be possible to remove this by first removing two or three fixing screws, but in most cases the plate has to be repeatedly twisted backwards and forwards until the thin pieces of metal holding it in place fatigue and break.

Cabling

The ribbon cable used to provide the data connection has three identical connectors. There is no specific connector for the motherboard and each drive, but because the cable is quite short it will probably have to connect everything together in a particular way in order to reach everything. It should not take too long to fathom out the best way of using the cable. Things are much easier when the new hard drive is the sole device on an IDE channel. The cable should then connect the motherboard to the drive without difficulty.

The connectors must be fitted to the motherboard and drives the correct way round. In theory the connectors are polarised and can only be fitted the right way round. There is a protrusion on the lead's connectors and a matching groove in the connectors on the motherboard and drives. Figure 3.6 shows the polarising keys in the two IDE connectors on a motherboard. Unfortunately, some connectors, and mainly those on motherboards, are sometimes a bit too minimalist and are not properly polarised. A search through the appropriate instruction manuals should show which is pin 1 on each connector. This information is often marked on the motherboard and the

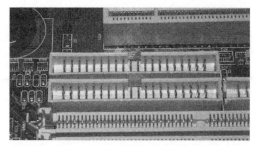

Fig.3.6 Two polarised IDE connectors on a motherboard

drives themselves. To make things easier, the ribbon cable has one red lead while the other 39 are grey. The convention is for the red lead to carry the pin 1 connection. Provided this lead is adjacent to pin 1 on the connector for the motherboard and both drives, everything will be connected together properly.

A spare power cable is needed for the new drive, and if there is a spare drive bay there should really be a spare power lead as well. However, it might be fitted with the smaller connector for 3.5-inch floppy drives, whereas it is the larger power connector that is required for hard disc drives, whether they are of the 3.5-inch or 5.25-inch variety. A large computer store should be able to provide a 3.5 to 5.25-inch power connector adapter. If there is no spare power cable, a splitter adapter is available. This provides two power connectors from a single power lead. Remove the power lead from the existing hard disc drive and connect it to the splitter. The two remaining connectors of the splitter are then connected to the hard disc drives. The power connectors are fully polarised and can only be connected the right way around. They are also quite stiff, and often need a certain amount of force in order to get them properly connected or disconnected again.

BIOS Setup

Having physically installed the hard disc it will be necessary to go into the BIOS Setup program and set the appropriate parameters for the new disc. The BIOS is something that most PC users never need to get involved with, but for anyone undertaking PC upgrading it is likely that some involvement will be needed from time to time. It is certainly something that can not be avoided if you add a second hard disc drive. In days gone by it was necessary to have a utility program to make changes to the BIOS settings, but this program is built into a modern PC BIOS. A modern BIOS Setup program enables dozens of parameters to be controlled, many of which are highly technical. This tends to make the BIOS intimidating for newcomers and even to those who have some experience of dealing with PC technicalities. However, most of the BIOS settings are not the type of thing the user will need to bother with, and very few are relevant to the hard disc drives.

BIOS basics

Before looking at the BIOS Setup program it would perhaps be as well to consider the function of the BIOS. BIOS is a acronym and it stands for basic input/output system. Its primary function is to help the operating system handle the input and output devices, such as the drives, and ports, and also the memory circuits. It is a program that is stored in a ROM on the motherboard. These days the chip is usually quite small and sports a holographic label to prove that it is the genuine article (Figure 3.7). The old style ROM is a standard ROM chip in the much larger DIL (dual in-line) encapsulation.

Either way its function is the same. Because the BIOS program is in a ROM on the motherboard it can be run immediately at start-up without the need for any form of booting process. It is the BIOS that provides the test procedures when a PC is switched on, and the BIOS also starts the boot process.

The BIOS can provide software routines that help the operating system to utilize the hardware effectively, and it can also store information about the hardware for use by the operating system, and possibly other

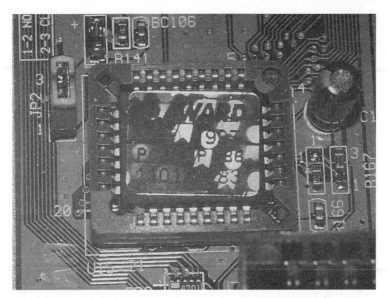

*Fig.3.7 A modern BIOS chip. This contains the Setup program in
        addition to the BIOS*

software. It is this second role that makes it necessary to have the Setup
program. The BIOS can actually detect much of the system hardware
and store the relevant technical information in memory. Also, a modern
BIOS is customised to suit the particular hardware it is dealing with, and
the defaults should be sensible ones for the hardware on the
motherboard. However, some parameters have to be set manually, such
as the time and date, and the user may wish to override some of the
default settings.

The Setup program enables the user to control the settings that the
BIOS stores away in its memory. A backup battery powers this memory
when the PC is switched off, so its contents are available each time the
PC is turned on. Once the correct parameters have been set it should
not be necessary to change them unless the hardware is altered, such
as a new hard disc drive being added or the existing hard disc being
upgraded. In practice the BIOS settings can sometimes be scrambled
by a software or hardware glitch, although this is not a common problem
with modern PCs.

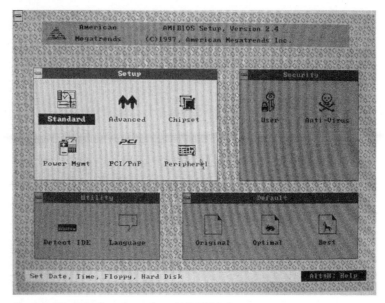

Fig.3.8 The initial screen of an AMI BIOS Setup program

Entry

In the past there have been several common means of getting into the BIOS Setup program, but with modern motherboards there is only one method in common use. This is to press the Delete key at the appropriate point during the initial testing phase just after switch-on. The BIOS will display a message, usually in the bottom left hand corner of the screen, telling you to press the "Del" key to enter the Setup program. The instruction manual should provide details if the motherboard you are using has a different method of entering the Setup program. The most common alternative is to press the "Escape" key rather than the "Del" key, but numerous alternatives have been used over the years, and no doubt some of these are still in use.

Every PC should be supplied with a manual that has a section dealing with the BIOS. Actually a lot of PCs are supplied with a very simple "Getting Started" style manual, but this is usually augmented by the manufacturers' manuals for the main components. It is then the motherboard manual that will deal with the BIOS. It is worth looking through the BIOS section of the manual before you actually go into the

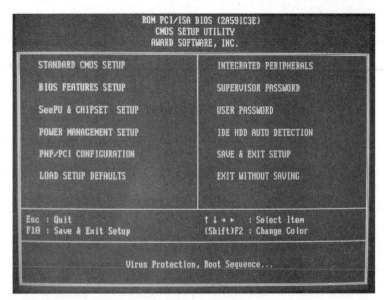

Fig.3.9 The initial screen of an Award BIOS Setup program

BIOS program. This will give you an idea of how things work, but do not bother too much about the more obscure settings.

In the current context it is only some of the Standard CMOS settings that are of interest. Do not expect the manual to give detailed explanations of the various settings. Most motherboard instruction manuals assume the user is familiar with all the BIOS features, and there will be few detailed explanations. In fact there will probably just be a list of the available options and no real explanations at all. This does not really matter, and you really only need to know how to get into the BIOS, make a few changes, save the changes, and exit the program.

There are several BIOS manufacturers and their BIOS Setup programs each work in a slightly different fashion. The Award BIOS and AMI BIOS are two common examples, and although they control the same basic functions, they are organised in somewhat different ways. A modern AMI BIOS has a Setup program that will detect any reasonably standard mouse connected to the PC, and offers a simple form of WIMP environment (Figure 3.8). It can still be controlled via the keyboard if preferred, or if the BIOS does not operate with the mouse you are using. The Award BIOS is probably the most common (Figure 3.9), and as far as I am aware it only uses keyboard control.

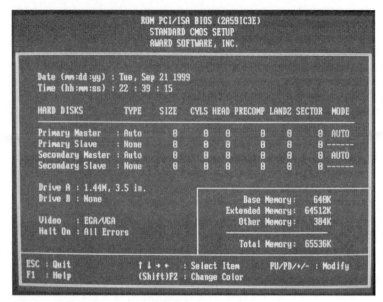

Fig.3.10 A typical standard CMOS Setup screen

Apart from variations in the BIOS due to different manufacturers, the BIOS will vary slightly from one motherboard to another. This is simply due to the fact that features available on one motherboard may be absent or different on another motherboard. Also, the world of PCs in general is developing at an amazing rate, and this is reflected in frequent BIOS updates. Fortunately, the Standard CMOS section has not changed much over the years, so it should not differ significantly from the one described here unless you are dealing with a computer than falls into the "antique" category.

Standard CMOS

There are so many parameters that can be controlled via the BIOS Setup program that they are normally divided into half a dozen or so groups. The most important of these is the "Standard CMOS Setup" (Figure 3.10), which is basically the same as the BIOS Setup in the original AT style PCs. The first parameters in the list are the time and date. These can usually be set via an operating system utility these days, but you can still alter them via the Setup program if you prefer. There are on-screen

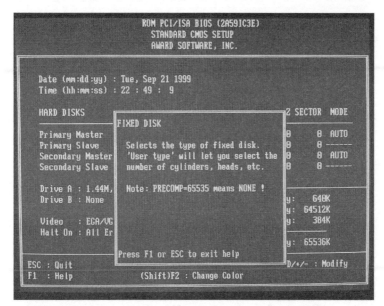

Fig.3.11 Most Setup programs provide context sensitive help

instructions that tell you how to alter and select options. One slight oddity to watch out for is that you often have to use the Page Up key to decrement values, and the Page Down key to increment them.

With virtually any modern BIOS a help screen can be brought up by pressing F1, and this will usually be context sensitive (Figure 3.11). In other words, if the cursor is in the section that deals with the hard drives, the help screen produced by pressing F1 will tell you about the hard disc parameters. It would be unreasonable to expect long explanations from a simple on-line help system, and a couple of brief and to the point sentences are all that will normally be provided.

Drive settings

The next section is the one we need, and it is used to set the operating parameters for the devices on the IDE ports. The hard disc is normally the master device on the primary IDE channel (IDE1), and the CD-ROM is usually the master device on the secondary IDE channel (IDE2). However, to avoid the need for a second data cable the CD-ROM drive is sometimes the slave device on the primary IDE interface. Your new drive could therefore be any of the four available devices apart from the primary device on IDE1, which will be the original hard disc drive. If in doubt, this table should help you decide which device it is:

IDE chan/device   If the new drive is...

IDE1 secondary   on the same cable as the original hard drive

IDE2 primary   the sole device on the opposite channel to the original hard disc

IDE2 secondary   on the same cable as the CD-ROM drive (or other device such as a CD writer)

Having decided how the new drive fits into the overall scheme of things you can set the appropriate parameters. The drive should really be supplied with a manual that provides the correct BIOS settings, but it is usually possible to get by without it. One of the parameters is the hard disc's type number. In the early days there were about 40 standard types of hard disc drive, and it was just a matter of selecting the appropriate type number for the drive in use. The BIOS would then supply the appropriate parameters for that drive.

This system was unable to cope with the ever increasing range of drives available, and something more flexible therefore had to be devised. The original 40 plus preset drive settings are normally still available from a modern BIOS, but there is an additional option that enables the drive parameters to be specified by the user. This is the method used with all modern PCs and their high capacity hard disc drives, so choose the Custom setting and ignore the drive numbers.

The drive table parameters basically just tell the operating system the size of drive, and the way that the disc is organised. Although we refer to a hard disc as a singular disc, most of these units use both sides of two or more discs. Each side of the disc is divided into cylinders (tracks), and each cylinder is subdivided into several sectors. There are usually other parameters that enable the operating system to use the disc quickly and efficiently. You do not really need to understand these parameters, and just have to make sure that the correct figures are placed into the drive table. As pointed out previously, the manual for the hard drive should provide the correct figures for the BIOS. If you do not have the manual, it can probably be downloaded from the disc manufacturer's web site.

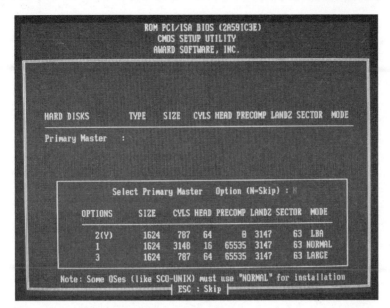

Fig.3.12 An IDE auto-detection screen

If you do not have the manual or prefer to take an easier option, a modern BIOS makes life easy for you by offering an "Auto" option. If this is selected, the BIOS examines the hardware during the start-up routine and enters the correct figures automatically. This usually works very well, but with some drives it can take a while, which extends the boot-up time. If the PC has been set up with this option enabled, the drive table will be blank.

There is an alternative method of automatic detection that avoids the boot-up delay, and any reasonably modern BIOS should have this facility. If you go back to the initial menu you will find a section called "IDE HDD Auto Detection" (Figure 3.12), and this offers a similar auto-detection facility. When this option is selected the Setup program examines the hardware on each IDE channel, and offers suggested settings for each of the four possible IDE devices. If you accept the suggested settings for the hard disc drive (or drives) they will be entered into the CMOS RAM. There may actually be several alternatives offered per IDE device, but the default suggestion is almost invariably the correct one. If you do not know the correct settings for a drive, this facility should find them for you.

It is perhaps worth mentioning that with an IDE drive the figures in the drive table do not usually have to match the drive's physical characteristics. Indeed, they rarely if ever do so. The electronics in the drive enable it to mimic any valid physical arrangement that does not exceed the capacity of the drive. In practice it is advisable to use the figures recommended by the drive manufacturer, as these are tried and tested, and should guarantee perfect results. Other figures can sometimes give odd problems such as unreliable booting, even though they are within the acceptable limits.

The last parameter for each IDE drive is usually something like Auto, Normal, LBA (large block addressing), and Large. Normal is for drives under 528MB, while LBA and Large are alternative modes for drives having a capacity of more than 528MB. Modern drives have capacities of well in excess of 528MB, and mostly require the LBA mode. The manual for the hard drive should give the correct setting, but everything should work fine with "Auto" selected.

It is increasingly common for modern motherboards to have four rather than two IDE interfaces. With a motherboard of this type it will usually be possible for the added hard disc drive to have its own IDE interface even if the PC already is already fitted with something like one hard disc drive, a CD-ROM drive and a CD writer. Finding a spare IDE channel for the new drive should be that much easier, but in other respects things are essentially the same as when dealing with a twin IDE port motherboard.

Drive letters

Some users get confused because they think a hard drive that will be partitioned should have separate entries in the BIOS for each partition. This is not the case, and as far as the BIOS is concerned each physical hard disc is a single drive, and has just one entry in the CMOS RAM table. The partitioning of hard discs is handled by the operating system, and so is the assignment of drive letters. The BIOS is only concerned with the physical characteristics of the drives, and not how data will be arranged and stored on the discs.

If you are adding a drive for backup purposes there is usually no point in using more than one partition. The only and fairly obvious exception if where the drive you are backing up has been partitioned to operate as two or more logical drives. It is then advisable to have the partitioning of the backup drive match that of the main drive as closely as possible.

The other Standard CMOS settings are concerned with the floppy discs and the default display type, and should simply be left as they are. The same is true of the settings in the other pages of the BIOS Setup program. Do not be tempted to start playing around with these unless you know exactly what you are doing. Entering silly settings is unlikely to damage anything, but could well prevent the PC from operating properly. The BIOS will probably have options that enable the previous settings to be reinstated, or default settings to be used. These can be useful if you should accidentally scramble a few parameters. Note though, that no settings are actually altered unless and until you select the Save Parameters and Exit option, and then answer Yes when asked to confirm this action. This is clearly the route you should take if everything has gone according to plan. Take the Exit Without Saving option if things have not gone well. Simply switching off the PC or pressing the reset button should have the same effect.

Partitioning

With the early PC hard disc drives it was necessary to do low level formatting of the drive before it could be partitioned and the high level formatting could be undertaken. Modern hard drives are supplied with the low level formatting already done. If there is a low level formatting option in the BIOS Setup program, never use it on an IDE hard disc drive. Do not use any similar facility in any utility suites that you might have.

No low level formatting is required, but with operating systems such as MS/DOS, Windows 95/98, and Windows Me the hard disc drive must be partitioned and high-level formatted before it can be used.

Start by booting the computer in MS/DOS mode, or from the floppy disc drive using a Windows Startup disc. If you do not have a Startup disc, one can be made by going into the Windows Control Panel. One route to this is to operate the Start button, and then select Settings and Control Panel. Once in the control panel double-click on the Add/Remove Programs icon, select Startup Disk, and finally operate the Create Disk button. Then follow the onscreen prompts. A blank 1.44 megabyte floppy disc is required. Note that you will be asked to insert the Windows 95/98/Me CD-ROM into the CD-ROM drive, because some of the files required are not normally stored on the hard disc. The method of making the disc is exactly the same for all three operating systems incidentally.

It is probable that the BIOS will already be set to boot from the floppy disc drive, but if necessary you must use the BIOS Setup program to set

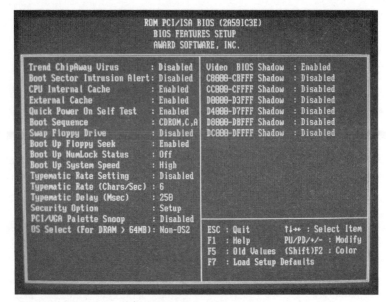

Fig.3.13 An example BIOS features Setup screen. Amongst other things, this is used to set the required boot option

the floppy drive as a boot device. There will be a page in the BIOS called something like BIOS Features Setup (Figure 3.13), and this should enable various boot sequences to be chosen. Choose one that has the floppy disc (drive A:) as the first boot device, and hard drive C: as the second. Any subsequent boot options are irrelevant, since the PC will always boot from one or other of the first two options.

With the computer booted-up and running MS-DOS or the Windows 95/98/Me equivalent of MS-DOS, the new hard drive will not be accessible. Until it has been partitioned it will be largely "invisible" to the operating system. Once partitioned the operating system will be more willing to admit to its existence, but it will still be of no use until high-level formatting has been performed using the MS-DOS FORMAT program. However, you must first prepare the disc using the FDISK partitioning program.

The Windows Startup disc contains copies of both FDISK and FORMAT, which are automatically placed on the disc for you when the Startup disc is created. Consequently, booting from the Startup disc is the easier way of doing things. If the PC is booted from the hard disc, either the Startup disc must be used to provide the FDISK and FORMAT programs, or you must find them on the hard disc. Unfortunately, they may not be present on the hard disc, or on the Windows CD-ROM in standalone form, so I would definitely recommend using the Startup disc. In the description that follows it is assumed that Format and FDISK are on the floppy disc in drive A:.

FDISK

FDISK is used to create one or more DOS partitions, and with discs of 2.1 gigabytes or less you may wish to have the whole of the disc as a single partition. Assuming the original hard disc has one partition, the new hard disc drive then becomes drive D:. By creating further partitions it can also operate as drive E:, drive F:, etc. The primary partition is the normally the boot disc, and this is where the operating system would be installed. Obviously this does not apply to a second hard drive, and the primary partition is simply the first partition on the disc.

The MS/DOS and Windows 95 file systems set the 2.1-gigabyte partition limit. There is also an 8.4-gigabyte limit on the physical size of the drive. With Windows 98 and any reasonably modern BIOS these limits do not apply, but you must use the FAT32 file system. To do this simply answer yes when FDISK is first run, and you are asked if you require support for large hard disc drives. Even if you do not wish to have a large disc organised as one large partition, it is still best to opt for large hard disc support. FAT32 utilizes the available disc space more efficiently and reduces wastage. Note that if you only require a single partition you must still use the FDISK program to set up this single partition, and that the FORMAT program will not work on the hard drive until FDISK has created a DOS partition.

Some hard discs are supplied complete with partitioning software that will also format the disc and add the system files, which will be copied from the boot disc. Where a utility program of this type is available it might be better to use it instead of the FDISK and FORMAT programs. These MS-DOS programs are fairly straightforward in use, but using the software supplied with the drive will almost certainly be even easier. The only problem is that the software might be intended for use with drive C:, and might give problems if you try to use it with drive D:. The instructions supplied with the software should make it clear whether the software is suitable for use with a second hard disc drive.

Should the program insist on placing the system files on drive D:, this is not really a major problem. The system files will waste a small amount of disc space, but should not give any problems when the system is booted provided the boot options are set correctly in the BIOS. If in doubt, simply use FDISK and FORMAT.

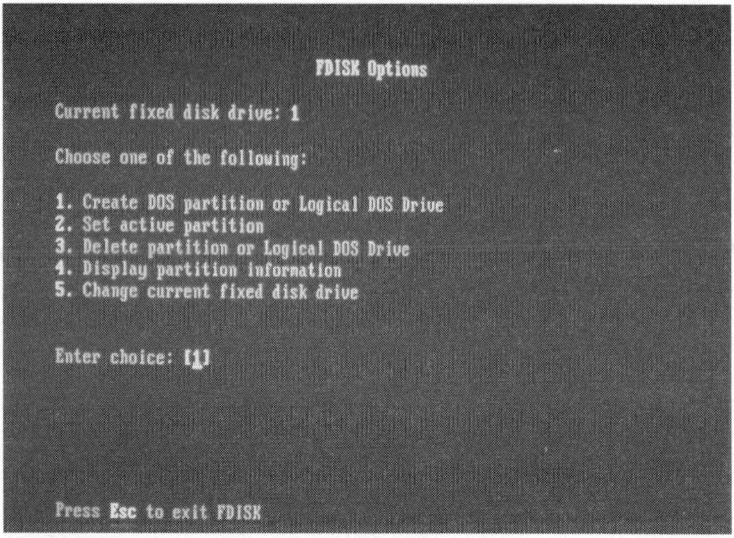

Fig.3.14 The main menu of the FDISK program

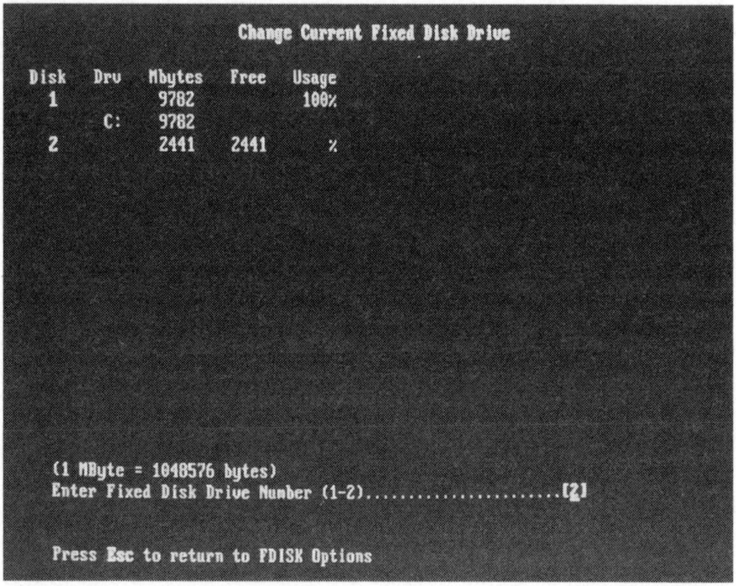

Fig.3.15 The partition information screen

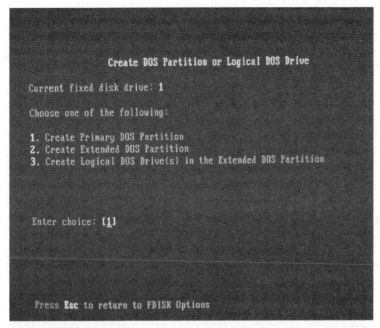

Fig.3.16 Creating a partition on the new hard disc

Using FDISK

Once you are in FDISK there is a menu offering these choices (see also Figure 3.14):

1. Create DOS partition or logical DOS drive

2. Set the active partition

3. Delete partition or logical DOS drive

4. Display partition information

5 Change current fixed drive

Normally the first thing we need to do is create a DOS partition using option one, which is the default. However, in this case we are dealing with an additional hard drive, and we must first make sure that it is the one FDISK is dealing with. It is very important that you do not accidentally use FDISK with the wrong drive, since to do so would almost certainly remove all the data from the disc you are trying to backup! Select option 5, which should bring up a screen like that in Figure 3.15. The original

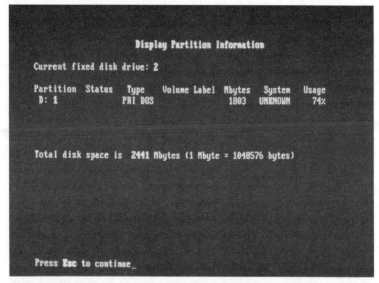

Fig.3.17 Checking that the new partition has been created

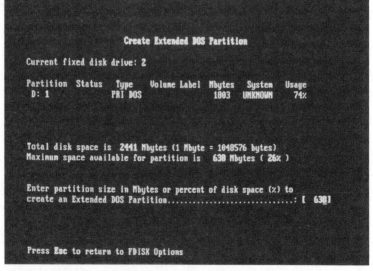

*Fig.3.18 Provided there is some spare capacity, one or more
additional partitions can be added*

hard disc unit is drive 1 and the new hard disc is drive 2. In this example drive 1 (C:) is the original drive of about 10 gigabytes in capacity, and drive 2 is the additional rescue drive having a capacity of about 2.4 gigabytes. Drive 2 will eventually be drive D:, but at this stage it has not yet been assigned a drive letter. If the current disc is drive 1, enter 2 for this parameter and press the Enter key to go back to the main screen.

Once drive 2 has been set as the current drive it can be partitioned, and option 1 can be selected. This takes you into a further menu offering these three options (Figure 3.16):

1. Create primary DOS partition

2. Create extended DOS partition

3. Create logical DOS drive(s) in the extended DOS partition

It is a primary DOS partition that is required, so select option one, which should again be the default. After the disc has been given a quick test you will be asked if you wish to use the maximum space for the partition. If you answer yes, the whole disc, or as much of it as FDISK can handle, will be used for the partition. If you answer no, you will then have to specify the size of the primary partition in megabytes. After a further quick check of the disc the new partition will be created. Having created the partition, press the Escape key to return to the original menu. It is a good idea to select option four to check that the partition has been created successfully (Figure 3.17).

If a further partition is required select option one, and then option two, which is "Create extended DOS partition" (Figure 3.18). Enter the size of the partition you require and press the Return key to create the partition. Then press the Escape key, which will bring up a message saying "No logical drives defined" (Figure 3.19). In other words, you have created a partition, but as yet it does not have a drive letter. Assuming you require all the space in the partition to be one logical drive, simply press the Return key. This will make the partition drive E:, and a screen giving this information will appear (Figure 3.20). Press the Escape key to return to the main menu, and use option four to check that the partition has been created successfully.

It has been assumed here that the original hard disc has a single partition. If it has more than one partition these will be drives C;, D;, etc., and the drive letter or letters for the additional drive will be moved up accordingly. For example, if the original disc is used as drives C: and D:, partitions of the new drive would become drives E:, F:, etc.

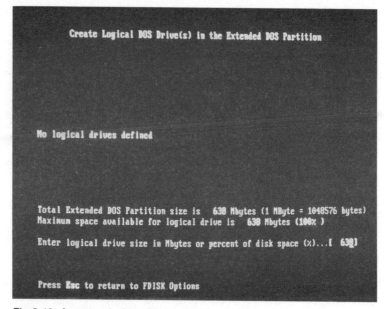

Fig.3.19 An extended partition must be given a drive number

Formatting

Having created the partitions you require, the "FORMAT" command can then be run. First you will have to press the Escape key twice to exit FDISK, and then the computer must be rebooted so that the new partition information takes effect. Make sure you format the correct disc, because formatting a disc that is already in use will destroy any data it contains. To format drive D: use this command:

format D:

This will bring up a warning to the effect that all data in drive D: will be lost if you proceed with the format. As yet there is no data to lose, so answer yes to proceed with the formatting. It might take several minutes to complete the task, since there are a large number of tracks to be processed and checked. If the hard disc has more than one partition and is operating as drive D:, drive E:, etc., each partition must formatted using a separate "FORMAT" command. To format drive F: for example, this command would be used:

format F:

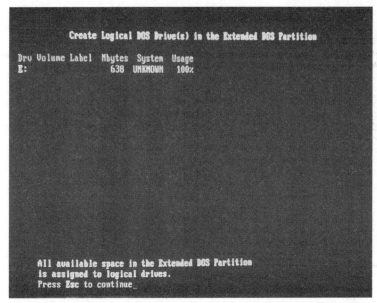

*Fig.3.20 If all goes well, a screen showing the drive letter of the new
partition will appear*

The new hard disc drive should then be fully operational. If the new disc
has been added as an insurance measure and the Windows installation
is fully operational, any backup software should be able to copy the
specified data from the old drive to the new one, or even copy every file
if that is what you require. Due to the speed of modern hard disc drives,
even copying several gigabytes of data should be relatively swift.

Matters are slightly less straightforward if the operating system is seriously
damaged and the second hard disc has been added as a desperation
measure. Any existing backup software already installed will probably
work well enough if the PC is booted into Safe Mode. With the CD-ROM
drive unavailable in Safe Mode, installing new backup software is
problematic. It is probably easier to run Windows Explorer and use this
to do the copying. Files or even complete directory structures can be
dragged and dropped from one disc to the other. Thus, even if there are
large numbers of files to copy in complex file structures, the task is not
too difficult.

Things would have to go disastrously wrong with the operating system
for Windows to be unable to boot in Safe Mode, but I suppose it could

happen if a lot of Windows files are damaged or erased. Copying single files using MS/DOS is easy enough, and is achieved using the Copy command. This is an internal command, which means that it is always available at the MS/DOS prompt, and does not rely on a program stored on disc. The easiest way of using the Copy command is to go into the directory where you require the copied files to be stored. Since the disc is blank to start with, the new directory must be created first. These two commands would first take the system into drive D:, and then make a directory (folder) called "wordproc" off the root directory of drive D::

D:

md wordproc

Of course, the Return key must be operated after each command has been typed in. Remember that in MS/DOS filenames directory names are limited to eight characters plus an optional three-character extension. These two commands would take the system into the new directory and then copy a file from drive C: into the new directory:

cd wordproc

copy C:\wordproc\letter1.doc

In this example the file being copied is called "letter1.doc" and it is in the "wordproc" directory of drive C:, but it can be any file on any directory of an accessible drive. The full path for the file must be specified, and not just the basic filename.

In most cases you need to copy all the files in a directory and not just one or two. This can be accomplished using this Copy command:

copy C:\wordproc*.*

The first "*" character tells the computer to apply the command to files having any filename. The second "*" character tells the PC to apply the command to files having any extension. Hence this easygoing version of the command will copy any files in the specified directory. A variation on this method enables any files with a specified extension to be copied. Suppose you wished to copy only the files having "doc" as the extension. This version of the command would give the desired effect:

copy C:\wordproc*.doc

The "*" character is used so that the command copies files having any main filename, but using "doc" as the extension ensures that only files having this extension are actually copied.

Xcopy

The Copy command is not able to copy a directory structure, complete with all subdirectories and the files that they contain. However, MS/DOS can accomplish this using the Xcopy command, but this is not an internal function of the operating system. In order for Xcopy to work the system must have access to the Xcopy program file (xcopy.exe). This file is available on the Windows 98 installation CD-ROM in the \TOOLS\OLDMSDOS subdirectory. It should also be on the hard disc in the \WINDOWS\COMMAND subdirectory. A quick search failed to locate the file on a Windows 95 installation CD-ROM, but it was present on the hard disc in the \WINDOWS\COMMAND subdirectory. The same is true of the Windows Me upgrade version, although the Xcopy.exe file can be located on the CD-ROM within the \Win9X\WIN_17.CAB file using Windows Explorer. However, it would seem to be easier to use the non-archived version of the file on the hard disc.

Suppose that you wish to copy a directory off the root directory of drive C:, plus any files and subdirectories it contains. There is more than one way of doing this, but the one I would recommend is to go into the directory that contains Xcopy.exe, and then specify the full paths for the source and destination. For example, to copy C:\wordproc to D:\wordproc, this command would be used:

Xcopy C:\wordproc D:\wordproc /s

Note that without the "/s" at the end of the command, Xcopy will work just like the Copy command and will not copy subdirectories.

Disc swap

There is another way of handling things where a Windows installation is damaged to the point that it will not even boot in Safe mode. This is to add the new drive as drive C:, and to have the original one as drive D:. This will probably require some changes to the cabling and jumper settings of the old drive, but it should not be too difficult to reorganise things so that the new drive is drive C:. The new drive is then set up as the boot drive, and Windows is installed on the drive once it has been partitioned and formatted. Your applications programs are then installed, and any data files on drive D: are easily copied across to drive C: using Windows Explorer.

The old drive then becomes the backup drive, and can be wiped clean once you are sure that any important data it contains has been copied to drive C:. Having cleared drive D:, it can be used to take a full backup of drive C:, which should make life much easier the next time a major Windows problem occurs.

Be prepared

It is definitely better to be ready for any problems that arise rather than having to improvise to get out of trouble when things go wrong. However, if the files you need to back up are safely stored on the hard disc, it should be possible to copy them even if the Windows installation has been damaged to the point where it is totally unbootable. You may need to add some hardware such as an external (parallel port) ZIP drive or a hard disc if there is a large amount of data to copy, but that is a small price to pay for saving large amounts of hard work.

Points to remember

Do not wait until things go wrong before backing up data. It should be possible to rescue your data if the operating system becomes seriously damaged, but it might be expensive to have it rescued from a faulty hard drive.

Data rescue services are available, but there is no guarantee that data will be retrievable from a damaged hard drive.

Not all backup devices will work with Windows in Safe mode or in MS/DOS. Lack of operation in either of these modes does not render a backup device useless, but life is easier when using a more accommodating drive.

If you find yourself with a Windows installation that seems to be impossible to repair, and no usable device to backup masses of important data, there are three options. Carry on trying to repair Windows for as long as it takes, abandon your data and reinstall Windows from scratch, or add a suitable backup device so that the data can be rescued prior to reinstalling Windows.

Another hard drive is the most practical option when disaster has struck and an emergency backup of data is required. These days a hard disc drive is a relatively cheap backup option that will work in both Safe mode and MS/DOS since it is a standard MS/DOS and Windows drive. Hard discs are also relatively fast in operation.

A modern PC can have at least four IDE drives (hard discs, CD-ROM drives, etc.) and will usually be able to accept an additional hard drive.

A hard disc drive has to be partitioned using FDISK and then high-level formatted using FORMAT before it is ready for use. These are both MS/DOS programs that are present on the Windows Startup disc. FDISK must be used even if the disc will be organised as one large partition. No low-level formatting is required, as this is done at the factory.

Proper backup software can be used to backup your data, but Windows Explorer enables data to be easily copied from one drive to another. Complete directory structures can be copied by dragging them from one drive to another.

Where Safe mode is not available the MS/DOS Copy command can be used to copy all the files from one directory to another. The MS/DOS Xcopy command can be used to copy directory structures and the files that they contain.

The easiest way of rescuing your data might be to fit a new C: drive and have the old one as drive D:. With Windows and all your applications software installed on drive C:, the old drive D: becomes the backup drive from which your data can be copied to drive C:.

Backup
and restore

Backup?

Using the methods outlined in the previous chapter it is possible to recover data from the hard disc when there is a serious problem with the operating system. Using a data recovery service it might even be possible to recover data from a faulty hard disc, albeit at a price. It is definitely advisable to avoid putting yourself into a situation where emergency measures have to be taken in order to avoid the loss of vital data, and this means backing up any important data. Of course, if you use a PC purely for pleasure and do not have any important data to back up, there will probably be little point in going to the trouble of backing up the hard disc. In the event of a serious problem everything can be reinstalled and there is no important data to lose.

These days most computer users are not dabblers, and their PCs are put to good uses. This means that important data is usually generated, and generated in large quantities. Whether it is family photographs from a digital camera, the company accounts, or your latest novel, most PCs contain data that is precious to the users. It makes sense to produce backup copies of this data, even if it does involve a certain amount of time and expense.

Better save than sorry

If you are going to do the sensible thing and backup important data it is not essential to use any backup software. Having stored a file onto the hard disc using the SAVE function of the application software you can simply select SAVE AS and store it again on another drive, such as a ZIP drive or CD writer. This method enables data files to be restored to the hard disc using Windows Explorer if a major failure of some kind should occur, but it does not allow the operating system to be restored. Neither will it restore any of your applications software or any customisation of that software. If the hard disc has to be replaced or the operating system becomes seriously damaged, the operating system has to be reinstalled, the applications programs are then installed again, and finally the data files are restored.

This is not a particularly quick or neat way of doing things, but for most users it will get the PC fully operational again in a reasonable amount of time. It has the advantage that it requires a minimal amount of time to maintain the backup copies, since only data files are being copied. As pointed out in previous chapters, it also gives you a "clean" copy of Windows that should operate quickly and efficiently.

If you use applications that only generate small amounts of data, an ordinary floppy disc drive is adequate for this method of backing up. Unfortunately, modern applications programs tend to generate large amounts of data. With a relatively simple application such as word processing the amounts of data generated might be reasonably small, but software such as graphics and desktop publishing programs usually produce large amounts of data. The folder used to store the files for this book will probably contain something like 500 megabytes of data by the time the book is finished. Backing up data requires some form of mass storage device when large files or large amounts of small files are involved.

Backup software

For anything beyond backing up data files it is best to resort to some sort of backup program. With these it is possible to save selected directories or directory structures, or the entire contents of the hard disc drive. Windows is supplied complete with a backup program that has the imaginative name of Backup. Although basic compared to some programs of this type it does the job well enough for most users. Its lack of popularity possibly stems from the fact that the equivalent facility in Windows 3.1 was something less than user friendly, causing many users to look elsewhere for a backup utility. Perhaps the problem is simply that the Backup program is a part of Windows that is easily overlooked. Anyway, it is easier to use than some of the earlier versions, and it is definitely there if you seek it out.

Backup is easily overlooked when using Windows 95, since it seems to be absent from a default installation. Backup is installed from the

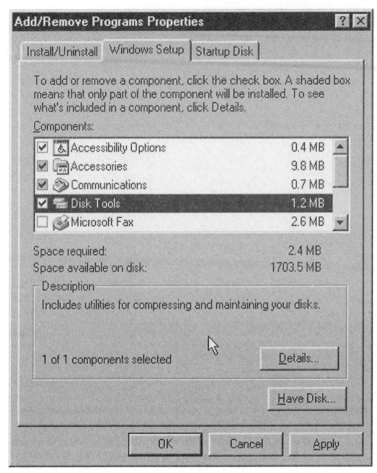

Fig.4.1 The Backup program is in the Disk Tools grourp

Windows Control Panel. First operate the Start button and then select Settings and Control Panel. Then double-click on the Add/Remove Programs icon and operate the Windows Setup tab of the window that pops up. Tick the box beside the Disk Tools entry (Figure 4.1) and operate the Apply button. Then follow the onscreen prompts to actually install the Backup program. Note that the Windows 95 disc will be needed during installation.

Fig.4.2 Adding the Backup program to Windows 98

If Backup is absent from Windows 98 it is added in much the same way as for Windows 95. Go into the Windows Setup program via the Control Panel as before, double-click on System Tools, and then check the box next to Backup. It may well be installed already, and the checkbox will already contain a tick mark (Figure 4.2) where this is the case. If the checkbox is ticked, operate the Cancel buttons to exit the Control Panel. If Backup is not already installed, operate the OK button and then the Apply button. Then follow the onscreen prompts to actually install the program. Have the Windows 98 disc handy as it will be required during the installation process.

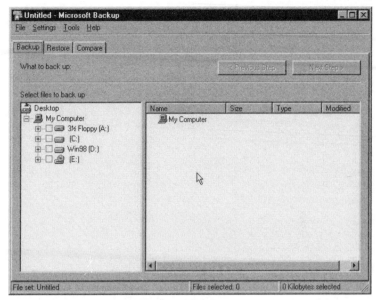

Fig.4.3 The Windows 95 version of Backup

Windows Me does have the Backup program but it is seems to have been included as something of an afterthought. Therefore, we will consider the Backup program of this version of Windows separately. In Windows 95 or 98 the Backup program is run from the Start menu by selecting Accessories, System Tools, and Backup. The two programs are not the same, and the biggest difference is that the Windows 95 version does not have Wizards to assist the user. It has an initial start screen that gives some basic information about using the program, and then the program itself appears (Figure 4.3). We will consider the Windows 95 version first.

When Backup is run it provides a message informing the user that a file set called Full System Backup has been created, and that this one must be used if a full backup of the hard disc drive is required. By default the program goes into the backup mode, and the first task for the user is to select the files that must be backed up. If a tick is placed in the checkbox beside drive C:, all the files on this drive will be selected. However, the left-hand section of the screen shows the files in the root directory, plus its sub-directories. These can be individually deselected and reselected by removing or replacing the ticks in their checkboxes. It is possible to

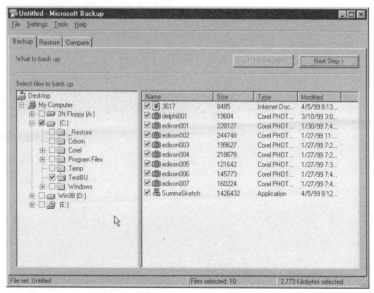

Fig.4.4 It is easy to select the files and folders that are to be backed up

navigate the directory structure in standard Windows fashion, removing and reselecting any files or directories, as required (Figure 4.4).

If you would like to do a simple dummy run to see how files are backed up and restored, make a new folder off the root directory and place some files in it. Limit the number and size of the files so that the new directory holds no more than two or three megabytes of data. One or two floppy discs can then be used for the backup copy, and the test should be reasonably quick. As only one directory is to be selected, do not tick the box for drive C: in the backup program and then deselect everything but the required directory. Instead, double-click on the entry for drive C: to expand it, and then place a tick in the checkbox for your test directory. The right-hand section of the screen will then show the files within that directory so that they can be individually chosen. For this exercise just leave them all selected.

Having selected the files to be backed up, the Next Step button is operated and this brings up a screen like the one in Figure 4.5. This enables the destination for the backup to be selected, and in this case floppy disc A: is being used. Left-clicking the mouse on the floppy disc's

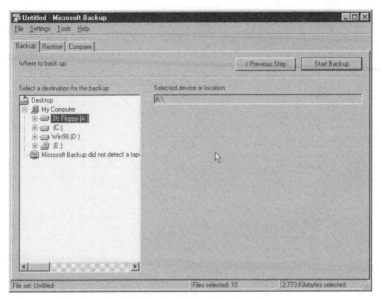

Fig.4.5 Selecting the destination for the backup copy

entry in the left-hand section of the screen will select it as the destination, and this should be confirmed by "A:\" appearing in the text box. Next the Start Backup button is operated and you will then be asked to provide a name for this set of backup discs. Having supplied a suitable name ("Test1" will do), operate the OK button and the program will start copying the files to the floppy disc drive.

In most cases the quantity of data being copied will be too large to fit onto a single floppy disc, CD-ROM, or whatever. The program will prompt you to change discs as and when necessary. The discs in multi-disc backup sets should be numbered in sequence. If you use re-writable discs that already contain data the Windows Backup program will be able to use them, but any existing data on the discs will be overwritten and lost. Once the process has been completed a message to that effect will appear on the screen, and you are then returned to the Backup program.

If you use Windows Explorer to examine the contents of the backup discs you will discover that they each contain one file. The name of this file will be the same for each disc, and it will be whatever name you

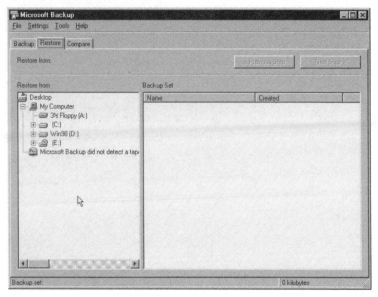

Fig.4.6 Specifying the source for the backup

assigned to the set of discs. This is not just of academic importance, and it means that the files stored on the disc can not be recovered simply by copying the contents of the discs back onto the hard disc drive. The only way of recovering the files is to use the Restore facility built into the Backup program.

To try out the restore feature, delete the test directory on the hard disc, run Backup, and then operate the Restore tab. This brings up the screen of Figure 4.6, which enables the source of the backup file to be specified. In this example we are using floppy drive A:, so this should be selected by left-clicking on its entry. The first disc in the backup set should be placed in drive A:, and the right-hand section of the window should confirm that the appropriate backup file is present on the disc. Next double-click on the entry for the backup file in the right-hand section of the screen. The left-hand section then changes to allow the files from the backup set to be selected.

In this example we will restore all the files, and this just requires the checkbox for the relevant directory to be ticked. Operate the Start Restore button to start the copying process, and change discs when directed by

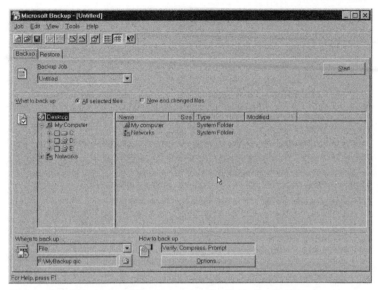

*Fig.4.7 The Windows 98 Backup program is similar to the
Windows 95 version*

onscreen prompts. A new window will appear while the files are being
copied, and this shows how far things have progressed. Once the
copying has been finished, operate the OK buttons to return to the
Backup program. Exit the program and then use Windows Explorer to
check that the directory and the files have been correctly restored.

Win 98 Backup

The Windows 98 Backup utility (Figure 4.7) is similar to the Windows 95
version, but has some additional facilities. Operating the Options button
towards the bottom right-hand corner of the screen brings up a window
(Figure 4.8) that enables various aspects of the program to be
customised. The main ones are that the files can be stored with no
compression or two degrees of compression, and password protection
can be used.

Using compression reduces the amount of storage space needed for
the backup copy. The amount of space saved depends on the nature of
the files being stored. Program and some types of data file will often

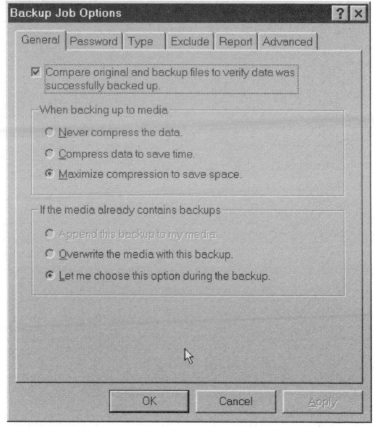

Fig.4.8 The options section of the Backup program

take up less than a third as much space, but something like a graphics file that is already heavily compressed is unlikely to benefit significantly from using further compression. Overall the files might be reduced in size by about 50%, which is certainly worthwhile. Apart from reducing the number of discs needed to store the backup copy, compression can significantly speed up both the backup and restoration processes.

Despite the advantages, some users prefer not to use compression. This is due to the fact that recovering data from a disc that has some minor corruption of the contents can be very difficult or impossible if compression has been used. This is not to say that data is easily recovered when a non-compressed disc becomes corrupted. There is no guarantee of success either way, and ideally two backup copies should be made where a hard disc contains very important data.

Another refinement of the program is that the radio buttons towards the top of the screen enable the user to opt for a full backup, or to only backup new files or ones that have changed since the previous backup was carried out. Obviously this second option is only applicable if a previous backup set has been made, and it can greatly speed up the process of maintaining up to date backup copies.

Wizards

Another refinement of the Windows 98 version of the program is that it has the option of using Wizards to control its operation. The Wizards are used by default when the program is run, and the process starts with the initial window of Figure 4.9, which enables the required function to be selected. If you do not wish to use a Wizard, simply operate the Close button and you will then be left with the unaided Backup program. If you wish to proceed using a Wizard, select the required function

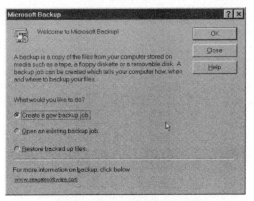

Fig.4.9 The first Wizard when using the Windows 98 Backup program

using the radio buttons and then press the OK button. The options are the normal backup and restore, plus an option to open an existing backup set. When first running the program a backup copy must be made, so the Backup option should be selected.

This launches the Backup Wizard, and the initial screen of Figure 4.10 appears. This gives the option of copying all files on the disc or just selected files. Once the required files have been selected or the "all files" option has been taken, the next Wizard (Figure 4.11) appears.

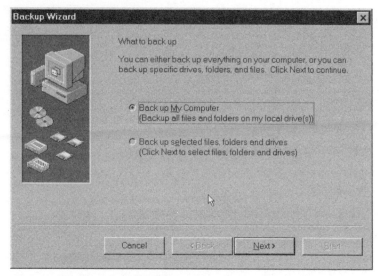

Fig.4.10 The Backup Wizard gives the option of making a full backup
or copying selected files

Here you choose whether to backup all the selected files or only those
that have been added or changed since the last backup was made.
Only the all files option is relevant when an initial backup is being made.

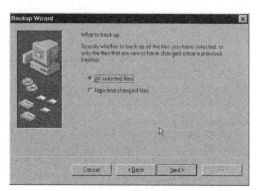

Fig.4.11 There is the option of backing up
all the files or only those that have
changed since the last backup

The next window
(Figure 4.12) is used
to   select   the
destination for the
backup copy. Note
that you must specify
a drive and a filename
and not just a drive
letter.

Next you are given
two options relating to
how the backup copy
is processed (Figure
4.13). The first one
enables verification to
be used. In other
words, the saved

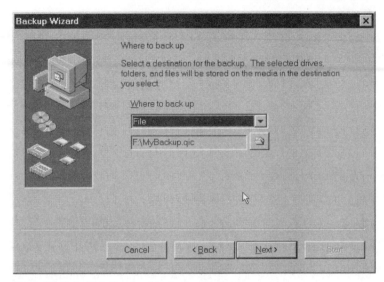

Fig.4.12 Selecting the backup's destination

copy can be compared to the original to make sure there are no copying errors. This is the safer option, as it should avoid the possibility of finding that a corrupted backup set can not be restored properly. The downside is that the verification process will result in the backup process taking significantly longer. Using verification is probably worth the extra time involved. The second button enables compression to be used if desired. I opt to use compression, but you

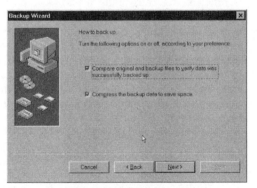

Fig.4.13 Verification and compression options are available

may prefer not to if only a modest amount of data is being copied, or if you have a large and fast backup medium.

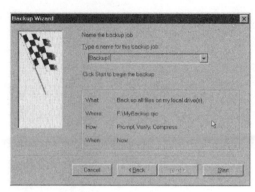

Fig.4.14 The backup must be given a name

The next window (Figure 4.14) is used to give a name to the backup job. This window also shows the settings that have been selected previously so that you can check that everything is set up correctly. The Back buttons can be used to retrace your steps if you change your mind about something, or to correct any mistakes. Simply press the Start button to begin the backup process. Restoration of a backup is an equally straightforward process using the Wizard method. Even if you are familiar with backup programs, it is probably easier to use the Wizards rather than opt for direct control of the program.

Emergency restoration

An obvious drawback of the Windows 95 and 98 Backup programs is that they are strictly Windows programs, and files can only be restored if the computer can be booted into Windows. In some circumstances it could be better, or even essential, to restore the files from MS/DOS. This is actually possible using Windows 98 via a batch file on the installation CD-ROM. The backup copy is made from Windows in the normal way, using the Backup program. This method of restoration will only work with a full backup incidentally. Bear in mind that it will only be possible to restore the files from MS/DOS if the backup medium is one that can be read from MS/DOS. The easiest options are a hard disc or CD-ROMs. If using the latter, ordinary CD-R discs are better than CD-RW discs, since the latter are usually only readable using a special utility program. This utility is usually a Windows program, and it is unlikely that a MS/DOS version of the utility will be available.

In order to restore a backup copy the computer must be booted using the Windows 98 Startup disc, and CD-ROM support should be selected when the menu appears. Next place the Windows 98 installation disc in the CD-ROM drive, and then set that drive as the current one. The Startup

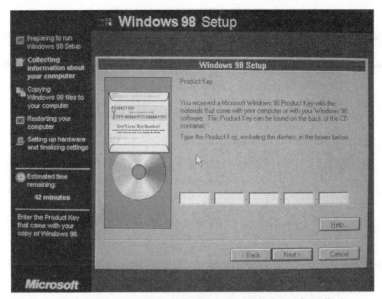

*Fig.4.15 The restoration starts with Windows 98 being reinstalled.
Here the product key is entered*

disc places some utilities on a virtual disc that is actually part of the
computer's memory. This will usually be given a drive letter ahead of
the CD-ROM drive, which is therefore shifted up one letter from normal.
For example, if the CD-ROM drive is normally drive E:, it will become
drive F: when the Startup disc is used. To move the system into drive F:
simply type "F:" and then press the Return key. A batch file in the
tools\sysrec directory controls the restoration process, so the next step
is to move the system into this directory using this command:

cd tools\sysrec

There is a text file called Recover.txt in this directory, and this gives useful
information about the recovery process. To run the batch file use this
command:

pcrestor

This may look incorrect, but it will not work if you add the missing "e" to
the command. MS/DOS only permits filenames of up to eight characters
plus a three-character extension. Hence this command is called
"pcrestor" and not "pcrestore". This brings up a message on the screen,
and then the Windows Setup program is started. After some checking

and initialisation you are presented with the screen shown in Figure 4.15, where your Windows 98 product key is entered. It is then just a matter of using the Setup Wizard to go through the installation and restoration process. This really just seems to be a variation on a normal Windows 98 reinstallation process, but it is probably best to do things this way if Windows is to be reinstalled followed by a full restoration of the hard disc.

Me Restore

As pointed out previously, Windows Me does not have the Backup program as standard, although it is still there if you care to unearth it from the installation CD. Instead it has a program called System Restore. It has to be emphasised that this is not a conventional backup program, and it can not be used to make a set of backup discs for use in the event of a hard disc failure. This is simply because it uses the hard disc to store the backup files, and if the hard disc fails, the backup files are inaccessible. System Restore is designed specifically to deal with problems in the operating system, and a separate backup utility is required to deal with hard disc failures.

This book is primarily concerned with fixing or working around problems that occur with the Windows operating systems, so the System Restore program is one that is fully relevant. Its purpose is to take the system back to a previous configuration. It is therefore a program that will work around problems rather than fix them. The general idea is to periodically add new restore points so that if something should subsequently go wrong with the operating system, it can be taken back to a recent restore point. Incidentally, Windows adds restoration points periodically, so it is not essential to routinely add your own.

The main reason for adding your own restoration points is that there is increased likelihood of problems occurring. The most common example of this is adding a restore point prior to installing new software. If anything should go horribly wrong during the installation process, going back to the restoration point should remove the rogue program and fix the problem with the operating system. You can then contact the software publisher to find a cure to the problem, and in the mean time your PC should still be functioning properly.

When going back to a restoration point the program should remove any recently added programs, but it should leave recently produced data files intact. Of course, with any valuable data that has not been backed

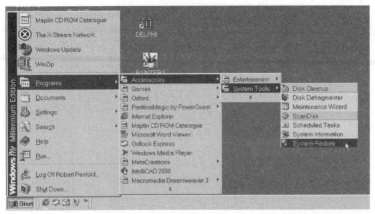

Fig.4.16 The System Restore program is deep in the menu structure

up already, it would be prudent to make backup copies before using System Restore, just in case things do not go according to plan. The program itself does provide a way around this sort of problem in that it does permit a restoration to be undone. If a valuable data file should vanish "into thin air" it should be possible to return the PC to its original configuration, backup the restored data, and then go back to the restoration point again.

In use

The System Restore program is buried deep in the menu structure (Figure 4.16), but it can be started by going to the Start menu and then selecting Programs, Accessories, System Tools, and System Restore. The program is controlled via a Wizard, so when it is run you get the screen of Figure 4.17 and not a conventional Windows style interface. The radio buttons give three options, which are to go back to a restoration point, create a new one, or undo the last restoration. When the program is run for the first time there is no restoration to undo, so this option will not be present.

As pointed out previously the system will automatically create restoration points from time to time, but you will probably wish to create your own before doing anything that will make large changes to the system. Start by selecting the "Create a restore point" option and then operate the Next button. The next screen (Figure 4.18) asks the user to provide a name for the restore point, and it is helpful if the name is something that

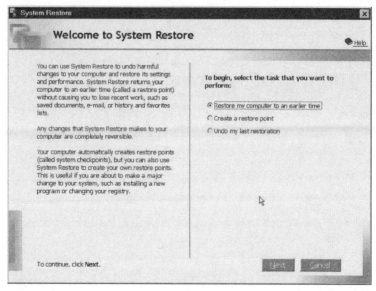

Fig.4.17 The welcome screen of the System Restore program

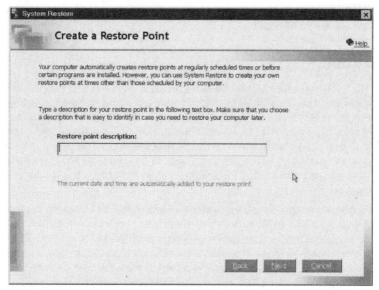

Fig.4.18 The system creates restore points, but you can add your own

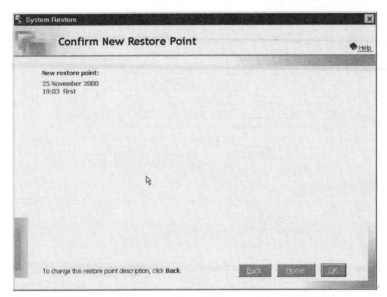

Fig.4.19 You have a chance to check things before creating a restoration point

will be meaningful. There is no need to bother about including a date, as the program automatically records the date and time for you.

There will be a delay of at least several seconds when the Next button is pressed, and then a screen like the one shown in Figure 4.19 will appear. This gives you a chance to check that everything is correct before the restoration point is created. If everything is all right, operate the OK button to create the restoration point and terminate the program.

To go back to a restoration point, run the program as before, and select the Return my computer to an earlier time option. Operate the Next button, and after a short delay a screen like the one of Figure 4.20 will appear. If there are a number of restore points available you can use the arrow heads in the calendar to find the one you require. The dates on the calendar in larger text are the ones that have restore points. Left clicking on one of these will show the available points in the screen area just to the right of the calendar. Left-click on the required restore point and then operate the Next button. This brings up a screen and warning message, like Figure 4.21. Left-click the OK button to remove the warning message, and close any programs that are running.

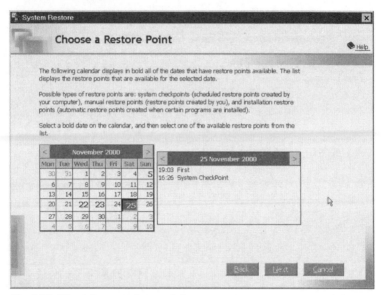

Fig.4.20 Choosing a restore point

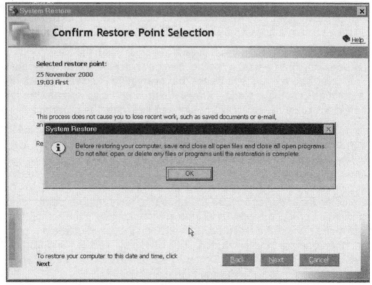

Fig.4.21 A warning message gives you a chance to change your mind

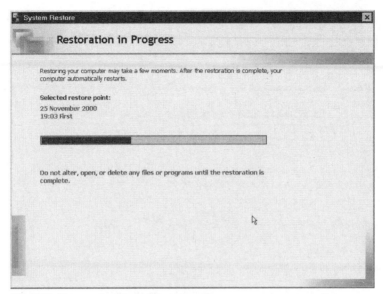

Fig.4.22 You can see how the restoration process is proceeding

If you are satisfied that the correct restore point has been selected, operate the Next button and the program will begin the restoration process. A screen showing how things are progressing will appear (Figure 4.22). Heed the warning on this screen, and do not do anything that will alter, open or delete any files while the program is running. Just sit back and do not touch the computer until the program has finished its task. Once the restoration has been completed the computer will reboot, and a message will appear on the screen (Figure 4.23). This confirms the point to which the computer has been returned, and indicates the options if the PC fails to operate properly using this restore point. Left-click the OK button to finish the boot process, and the computer should then have shifted back in time to the appropriate restoration point.

Windows Me is still relatively new at the time of writing this, but the System Restore utility certainly seems to be a very worthwhile facility. Some consider that this feature alone justifies upgrading from Windows 95 or 98. To date I have only used it a few times in earnest, but it certainly provided the desired result on each occasion. It is probably not a good idea to use the System Restore program as a first resort if there is a

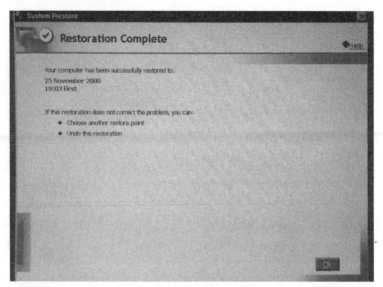

*Fig.4.23   Once the restoration has been completed the computer will
reboot. This message appears after the reboot is finished*

problem with the operating system, but it is certainly worth a try where
the problem has no simple solution.

Me Backup

If you wish to use the Windows Me Backup program it is no good trying
to install it via the usual Windows Setup section of the Control Panel. It
no longer seems to be a standard Windows component that can be
installed via the usual route. Instead, you must use Windows Explorer
to delve into the Windows Me installation disc. Go into the Add-ons
folder and then into the MSBackup folder. Here you will find a text file
called backup.txt and a program called msbexp.exe. To find out more
about installing and uninstalling the Backup program double-click on
the entry for the text file. In order to install the program it is just a matter
of double clicking on the entry for msbexp.exe and then following the
onscreen prompts. Once installed, the program can be run from the
Start menu via the usual route (Programs, Accessories, and System
Tools). The program seems to be much the same as the Windows 98
version, as can be seen from Figure 4.24.

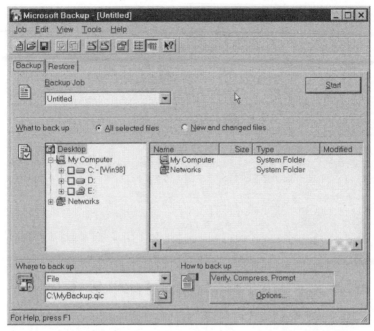

Fig.4.24 The Windows Me Backup program is much like the Windows 98 version

Backup programs

If you prefer not to use the built-in backup and restore facilities of Windows, or you would like to augment them, there are plenty of programs to choose from. These include various backup programs and software that restores the computer to an earlier configuration, rather like System Restore in Windows Me. One type of software that should not be overlooked is the type that copies the contents of one drive onto another, producing what is generally termed an "image" of the original drive. Although it might seem that simply copying the files from one disc to the other would produce an exact clone of the original, the clone would probably fail to boot. This is due to the fact that some of the system files have to be in the right place on the hard disc, and not merely present on it in order to make the drive bootable. If you simply require a backup copy of data files this is of no consequence, but it is a crucial factor if you require a drive that can be used in place of the original if disaster strikes.

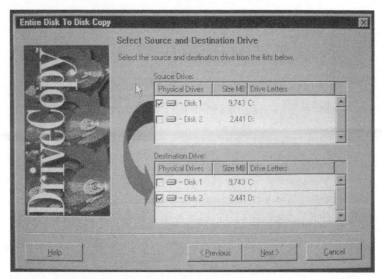

*Fig.4.25 "Cloning" a hard disc drive is easy using a program such as
Drive Copy*

It is actually possible to make a bootable copy of a hard disc drive using
the MS/DOS Xcopy program, but it requires just the right switches to be
used in the Xcopy command and other factors also have to be just right.
The process can also be very slow when applied to some PCs. A program
designed specifically for producing drive images will usually do the job
much more quickly and easily. Probably the best known program of
this type is Drive Copy, which is shown in action in Figure 4.25. This
program is supplied on CD-ROM, but it is used to make a bootable
floppy disc that is used when undertaking the copying. You have to do
little more than make sure that the program is copying the data in the
right direction, and then sit back while it makes the copy.

Once you have a clone of the original hard disc it can either be removed
from the PC and stored away safely or it can be left in place as drive D:.
Storing the drive has the advantage that the disc will not be subject to
wear, and it should be ready and working if it is needed at some later
date. On the other hand, the drive will not be subjected to significant
wear if it is just sitting in the PC getting little or no use. The drive motor
will be operating while the PC is in use, but the motors are very reliable
and can be expected to last a very long time. Another advantage of
removing the drive is that the data it contains can not be accidentally

corrupted. This avoids the slight risk that when switching to the backup drive it does not work any better than the one containing the damaged Windows installation.

The obvious advantage of keeping the drive in place is that it is ready for immediate use if the main drive should fail or the Windows installation becomes damaged. With most PCs it is possible to go into the BIOS and set drives D:, E:, or F: as the boot drive, so it should be possible to boot into the standby drive. This could be useful in trying to fix the operating system on the main drive and in backing up data if Windows has to be installed "from scratch". For instance, all the drives including things like CD writers and re-writers should be fully operational when booting from the standby drive.

Another advantage of keeping the standby drive in place is that it can be used to backup data files as they are produced, so that a failure of the main drive will cause no loss or a minimal loss of data. However, using the standby disc does increase the risk of its contents becoming corrupted so that it no longer bootable.

There are various backup programs available that can be used as an alternative to the Windows Backup program. Some of these will monitor disc activity and make automatic backup copies when new files are generated or existing files are altered. These are very convenient in use because they are largely "transparent" to the user, but they run continuously in the background and add to the drain on the computer's resources.

System files

If Windows becomes troublesome due to a missing or damaged system file, life is a lot easier if you have a backup copy of the file in question. One of the main causes of problems are DLL (dynamic link library) files, which are used extensively by Windows and applications programs. DLL files provide program code for frequently performed functions, such as displaying menus and dialogue boxes. Some are supplied as part of the Windows operating system, while others are loaded onto the hard disc when applications programs are installed.

Reinstalling a standard DLL file from the Windows installation disc should not be difficult, but one installed by an application program could be more difficult to replace. Firstly, you might not know which program supplied the file. The second problem is that searching the relevant CD-ROM for the file might not be successful. Files are often stored on installation discs in some form of compressed or archived form, making it difficult to locate and extract the one you require.

The DLL files are likely to be liberally spread across the hard disc, but using Windows Explorer it is easy to locate all of these files and copy them to a mass storage device such as a CD-ROM writer. The amount of storage space required will vary considerably from one Windows installation to another, and the more applications that are installed the more DLL files there will be. Backing up the DLL files on one of my PCs required some 500 megabytes or so of storage space, which is probably quite typical.

In order to copy the DLL files launch Windows Explorer and then select Find and Files or Folders from the Tools menu. Enter "*.dll" as the filename, and then make sure that drive C: is entered in the Look In box and that the "search subfolders" checkbox is ticked. The "*" character in the filename tells the search program to accept anything as the main part of the filename. When you operate the Find Now button, the program will therefore search for any file that has "dll" as the extension. You should end up with something like Figure 4.26, with a large number of DLL files listed in the lower section of the window. I am not exaggerating when I say that there will probably be a few thousand files listed! To highlight all the files go to the Edit menu and choose the Select All option. Then go to the Edit menu again a select Copy.

The DLL files can then be Pasted to a backup folder on the hard drive, a CD-R, or whatever, using Windows Explorer. If the files are to be stored on something like Zip discs that can not store all the files on a single disc, the copying process becomes more difficult. Batches of files must be highlighted manually and copied to the backup discs, being careful not to have any batch larger than the storage capacity of the disc. It is possible that during the copying process you will be asked whether or not to overwrite a file that has already been copied, with another file of the same name. The rule here is to not replace a newer file with an older version, so check the dates of the two files and proceed accordingly.

Obviously it could be very time consuming to manually search the backup disc or discs for a specific DLL file that you need. The quick way is to use the Find Files or Folders facility of Windows Explorer. This can search through thousands of files and locate the one you require in a few seconds. Having found the required file, the Copy and Paste facilities of Windows Explorer can be used to copy it to the appropriate folder on the hard disc.

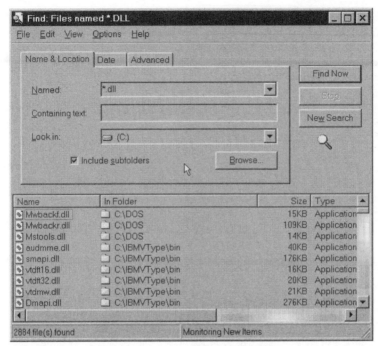

Fig.4.26 The Find Files or Folders facility of Windows Explorer can be used to find and copy all the DLL files on a hard drive

Registry backup

Although Windows makes its own backup copies of the Registry, some users prefer to have an additional backup copy. Since the file sizes involved are quite small it makes sense to keep the backup copies on floppy discs, a Zip disc, etc., rather than on the hard disc where they are vulnerable to disc failures. The Windows Registry sounds as though it should be a single file, but as explained in chapter 2, it is actually system data contained in two files called User.dat and System.dat. In order to backup these files it is merely necessary to locate them on the hard disc using Windows Explorer and then drag them to a floppy drive, Zip drive, or whatever.

Bear in mind that these are system files, and that using the default settings of Windows Explorer they are hidden from view. If you are going to undertake Windows troubleshooting the settings in Windows Explorer

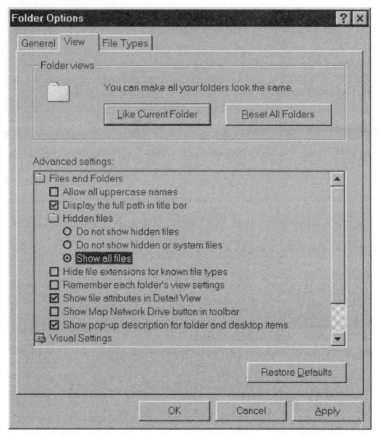

Fig.4.27 Windows Explorer can be made to show hidden files and other information that is not shown by default

should be such that the system files are visible anyway, but it is essential if you are going to use Explorer to backup any of these files. Activate the View menu and then select Folder Options. Operate the View tab of the new window that appears, which will produce a number of check boxes and radio buttons that can be used to select the desired options (Figure 4.27). Under the Hidden files section make sure that the Show all files radio button is selected.

The User.dat file is usually quite small and will fit onto a 1.44-megabyte floppy disc quite comfortably. The System.dat file tends to vary in size

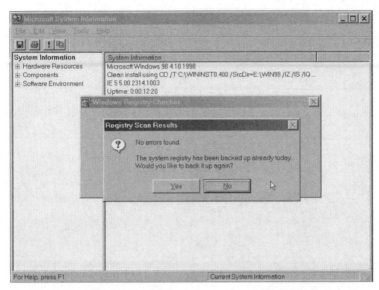

Fig.4.28 The Registry Checker can be used to make a backup of the Registry files

quite substantially from one PC to another, but in general it seems to be much larger and can be several megabytes in size. Even using compression it is unlikely that this file will fit on a single floppy disc, but there are programs that can spread large files across several floppy discs and reconstitute them again. For instance, later versions of the popular Winzip program can accomplish this. Alternatively, copy it to a larger disc such as a CD-R or Zip type.

Registry Checker

Of course, there are plenty of other Windows files that can be backed up, but these are less likely to be of use for a quick fix than the DLL and registry files. Two possible exceptions are system.ini and win.ini, both of which will be found on the boot disc in the Windows folder.

Windows does actually have a facility to backup and restore the Registry. Probably the main use of this feature is when undertaking something that involves a higher than normal risk of the Registry becoming damaged, which mainly means installing or uninstalling software, including the drivers for hardware. The Registry can be backed-up before

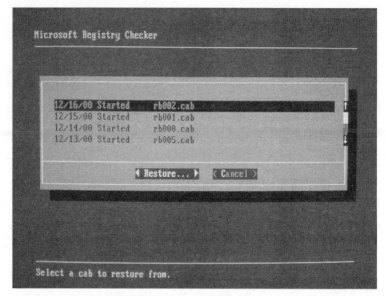

Fig.4.29 Restoring a backup copy of the Registry from MS/DOS

the software is installed or removed from the system, and restored again if things go awry. In order to backup the registry select Programs from the Start menu, followed by Accessories, System tools, and Registry Checker. The Registry Checker will look for errors in the Registry, but it will presumably fail to find any. It will then display the message of Figure 4.28. The last backup copy made by the system automatically is probably sufficient, but operate the Yes button to ensure that there is a fully up to date backup copy of the Registry.

The Registry Checker runs automatically each time the computer is booted, and it will ask for confirmation that you wish to resort to a backup copy if the Registry is found to be damaged. It makes sense to restore an earlier version of the Registry when major corruption has been detected, since there is no chance of the computer booting successfully using the corrupted Registry. The Registry Checker program will not always detect a problem in the Registry, and it is mainly designed to find something fairly major such as part of the file being obliterated. Consequently, the Registry Checker may fail to find any problems but a Registry fault could still result in the computer failing to boot properly.

If the system fails to boot properly, perhaps after some software has been installed or removed, boot into MS/DOS. Booting from drive A:

using a Windows Startup disc or from C: using MS/DOS mode are both acceptable in this case. Next type this command and press Return, which will produce a screen like the one in Figure 4.29:

C:\windows\command\scranreg /restore

This command includes the full path to the Scanreg program, so the system does not have to be in a particular drive or directory when it is issued. By default, Windows keeps five copies of the Registry, but this includes the one that is currently in use. This screen enables any of the four backup copies to be restored. Thus, if the most recent backup is faulty, you can revert to an earlier version and try again. Use the up and down cursor keys to select the backup copy you require and then press enter. If you change your mind and do not wish to reinstate a backup copy of the registry, press the right cursor key to highlight the Cancel option and then press Return.

The backup copies of the Registry files can also be restored from within Windows. The backup copies are stored in cabinet files in the \Windows\sysbckup folder, but this is a hidden folder so it will only be visible to Windows Explorer if it is set to show hidden files and folders. There are several cabinet files in this folder (the ones having a "cab" extension), and the dates of the files indicate the ages of the backup copies that they contain. To restore a pair of backup files they are extracted from the cabinet file and copied to the main Windows directory. The existing Registry files will have to be overwritten so answer "yes" if you are asked if you wish to overwrite them.

System File Checker

Although Windows 98 does not have a true equivalent to the System Restore facility of Windows Me, the System File Checker does provide a similar but more restricted restore facility. Unfortunately, this facility can go seriously wrong using the original version of Windows 98, so it is best not to use it unless you are using Windows 98 SE. In order to run the System File Checker select Programs from the Start menu, followed by Accessories, System Tools, and System Information. Then select System File Checker from the Tools menu of the window that appears. This will produce the window shown in Figure 4.30.

Use the default settings and operate the Start button. The program will then scan the disc, recording a list of system files and checking that they are in good working order. If all goes well, System File Checker should produce an onscreen message stating that the scan has been

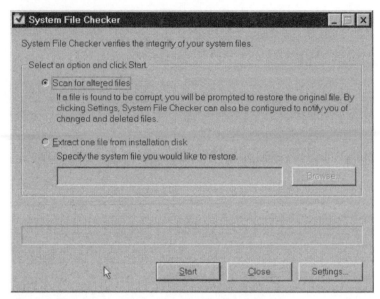

Fig.4.30 The initial screen of the System File Checker

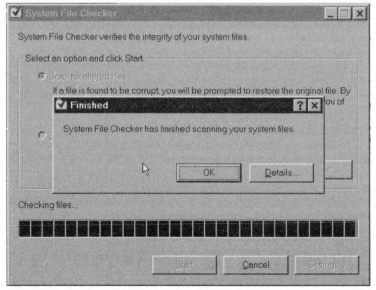

Fig.4.31 A message is produced when the check has been completed

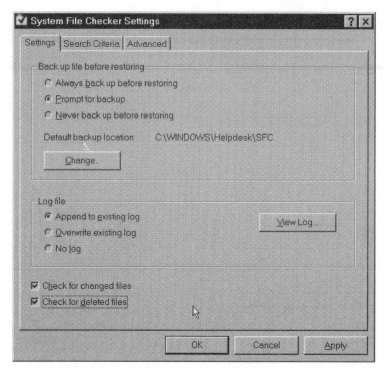

Fig.4.32 The Settings screen of the System File Checker program

completed successfully (Figure 4.31). Suppose that you now install or uninstall some software and Windows is left with a problem or two. Run System File Checker again, but this time operate the Settings button to bring up a screen like the one in Figure 4.32. Put ticks in both the check boxes towards the bottom of the window so that System File Checker will search for files that have been altered or deleted since the previous check. Operate the Apply and OK buttons to make the new settings take effect, and then run System File Checker again.

A warning screen like the one of Figure 4.33 will appear if a file is missing or has been altered since the previous time the program was run. You then have several options available. Clearly the Ignore option should be chosen if you have reason to believe that the file in question has been correctly changed or deleted. If the file is one that is on the Windows installation disc and it is not one that has been deliberately changed or deleted, the obvious choice is to restore the file.

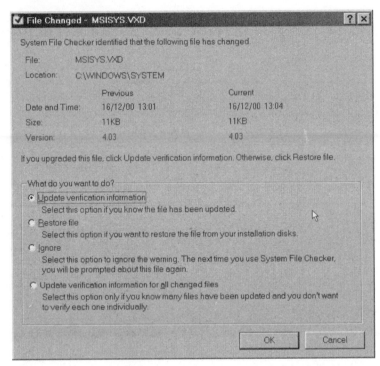

Fig.4.33 The user is warned if a file has been altered or deleted

To do this, first left-click on the Restore file radio button and then operate the OK button. A Window with two dialogue boxes will then appear (Figure 4.34). The default destination should be correct, but you will

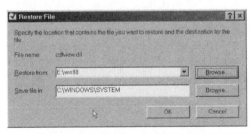

Fig.4.34 Selecting the source and destination when replacing an altered file

either have to type in the path for the source or use the Browse feature to locate it. It is not necessary to point the program directly to the missing file, which will probably be hidden away inside a cabinet file anyway. Just direct it to the drive that contains the Windows 98 installation disc, and the correct folder on that disc. This will usually be the Win98 folder. The missing or corrupted file should then be replaced, and the program will continue with its checking process.

Points to remember

Backing up data and (or) system information to another drive is the only way to guard against a hard disc failure. Backing up system information to the main hard drive is sufficient to guard against problems with the operating system.

Floppy discs are inadequate to cope with the large amounts of data produced by many modern applications. A CD writer, Zip drive, additional hard disc, or some other form of mass storage device is required. A mass storage device is also required in order to make a full backup of the main hard disc drive.

It is only necessary to save important data and configuration files, but it is much quicker to get things back to normal if you make a full backup of the hard drive.

Plenty of third party backup software is available, but the Windows Backup utility is adequate for most purposes. It is included with Windows 95, 98, and Me, but is not necessarily included as part of the default installation. In fact it has to be "dug out" from the installation CD-ROM with Windows Me.

The Windows Backup program can be used to backup selected files, or a full backup of the hard disc can be provided. Backing up the full contents of a hard disc can be time consuming, but restoring a full backup is the quickest way to get the computer into full working order again if a major problem occurs.

Windows Me has a System Restore program that can be used to take the system back to the way it was at some previous time. Using System Restore to take the system back a day or two will usually remedy boot problems, etc.

Windows 95 and 98 lack a System Restore facility, but there are other facilities that provide a similar effect and will often cure Windows problems. The simplest approach is to revert to one of the backup copies of the Registry. In Windows 98 the System File Checker can be used to check for altered or deleted system files and to make repairs.

It is worthwhile making a backup copy of all the DLL files on the hard disc. In the event of a DLL file becoming deleted or overwritten by an older version, the original is easily found and reinstated. It is worthwhile backing up System.ini and Win.ini configuration files as well.

The Registry is stored in two hidden files called User.dat and System.dat. These are routinely backed up by the operating system, but it can be useful to store backup copies on floppy discs, a CD-R, etc.

If the computer will not boot into Windows, backup copies of the Registry can be restored using the Scanreg program with the computer booted into MS/DOS. Of course, your own backup copies can be restored in MS/DOS using the Copy command.

5

Reinstallation

Clean sweep

Having decided to install Windows and your applications from scratch, and having also done any necessary backing up of data files, etc., it is time to start the reinstallation process. I would not recommend trying to reinstall Windows by booting into Windows. If you can only boot Windows in Safe Mode there will be no CD-ROM support, so it will not be possible to install Windows from the installation CD-ROM. Even if the PC can be booted into a largely working version of Windows, an installation started from Windows will simply place the new version on top of the old one, but it will not necessarily repair any problems in the existing Windows set up.

Unless you have definitely decided that it is time to "sweep away the cobwebs" and start from scratch, I would certainly recommend trying to fix Windows by reinstalling it on top of the broken version. If this fails to cure the problem it is time to install Windows from scratch. Either way, I would recommend booting from a Windows Startup disc in drive A: and selecting CD-ROM support when the menu appears. The difference is that when installing Windows "from scratch" it is necessary to wipe the hard disc clean first. When installing Windows over the existing version all the existing files on the hard disc are left in place. Simply run the Windows Setup program once the computer has booted into MS/DOS.

The basic installation process is much the same for Windows 95, 98, and Me. Although the description provided here is for an installation of Windows Me, the basic procedure is therefore much the same for Windows 95 and 98. Also, the process is much the same whether the operating system is installed from scratch or on top of an existing Windows installation. If Windows is already on the hard disc it will be detected by the Setup program, which will then reinstall it on top of the existing Windows installation, by default. Any Windows applications programs on the disc should remain properly installed with the new Windows installation.

It is because Windows finds any existing installation and merges the new version into it that an installation "from scratch" is sometimes needed. Completely wiping is the easiest way to ensure that there is no information left on the disc to lead the new installation astray. However, it also means that any data on the disc will be lost unless it is properly backed up. You can try a middle course with the Windows directory structure being deleted, but everything else being left on the disc.

With luck this will result in Windows being reinstalled successfully, and any problems in the old installation will not resurface. In practice there is no absolute guarantee of success though. Also, bear in mind that any Windows applications on the hard disc will not be installed in the new version of Windows. All the applications will therefore have to be reinstalled on top of the existing software. An advantage of this method is that any data files should be left intact, but note that configuration files for the applications programs will probably be overwritten when the programs are reinstalled.

Things can be taken a stage further, with the data files and any other important files being copied to a new folder. Everything else on the disc is then deleted and Windows is installed "from scratch". Where there is no other means of backing up important files, this method has the advantage that the files should still be intact once Windows has been reinstalled, and there are no system files, etc., left on the disc that could have a detrimental effect on the new Windows installation. Backing up important files to another disc is still preferable, because the backup copies on the main disc will be lost if there is a disc fault or a major problem during the Windows reinstallation.

If you decide to delete certain directories rather than simply wiping the disc clean, it is best to do most of the deleting in Windows using Windows Explorer. Using Windows Explorer it is possible to "zap" complete directory structures almost instantly. Deleting large numbers of files and directories in MS/DOS tends to be a very long, slow, and drawn out process.

The reinstallation process described here provides a true installation "from scratch", with the hard disc being wiped clean. However, the initial part of the process is easily modified to accommodate one of the alternative methods outlined previously. The main installation then proceeds in more or less the same fashion.

Booting up

The first task is to boot the computer from a Windows Startup disc. If you do not have a Startup disc, one can be made by selecting Settings from the Start menu, then Control Panel and Add/Remove Programs. Left-click on the Startup Disk tab, operate the Create Disk button, and then follow the onscreen prompts. With the Startup disc in drive A:, restart the computer and with luck it will boot using the Startup disc. The BIOS settings are unsuitable if the computer ignores this disc and tries to boot from the hard disc instead. In this event you must go into the BIOS and choose a boot-up option that has A: as the initial boot disc and drive C: as the second boot disc. Any subsequent boot options are irrelevant, because the PC will boot before it gets to them.

Once the PC starts to boot-up using the Startup disc you will be presented with a menu offering three or four choices. Select the one that boots the computer using CD-ROM support. This is important, because you can not run the Setup program on the Windows CD-ROM without the CD-ROM support. The CD-ROM support works with the vast majority of CD-ROM drives, including virtually all types that use an IDE interface. However, it does not work with all drives. If it does not work with the CD-ROM drive of your computer you must make your own boot disc with CD-ROM drivers.

To make a boot disc first boot the PC in MS/DOS mode. To do this you must operate function key F8 as the system starts to boot into Windows, and then select the appropriate option from the menu that appears. Once the computer has booted into MS/DOS put a blank disc in drive A: and issue this command:

format A: /s

This will format the disc and add the system files needed to make it bootable. In Windows Me there is no option to boot in MS/DOS mode, but the computer can be booted using a Startup disc, and then this command can be used:

format B: /s

In the unlikely event that your PC has a drive B:, this will format the disc in drive B: and place the system files onto it. If there is no drive B:, the operating system will use drive A: as both drive A: and drive B:, and you will have to do some disc swapping when indicated by the onscreen instructions. The CD-ROM and mouse drivers should then be installed onto the floppy disc. The PC should have been supplied with this driver software, together with instructions for using the installation programs.

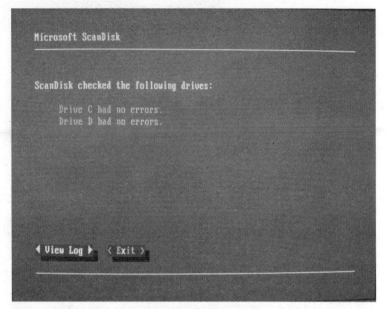

*Fig.5.1 The MS/DOS version of Scandisk is run automatically as the
initial stage of the Setup routine*

Once this has been done the PC should be rebooted, and it should then
be possible to access the CD-ROM drive.

It is necessary to wipe everything from the hard disc if Windows and the
applications programs are to be installed from scratch. The easiest way
of achieving this is to reformat the hard disc. It will presumably be drive
C: that will take the new installation, so this command would be used to
format this disc:

format C:

It does not seem to be necessary to have the system files placed on the
disc, and they are presumably added by the Windows Setup program
during the installation process. The "/s" switch is therefore unnecessary,
although adding it will not do any harm. Before formatting the disc the
program will warn that all data on the disc will be lost. Make sure that all
important data has been backed up properly before the disc is
reformatted.

Fig.5.2 The welcome screen of the Windows Setup program

Windows Setup

Once the mouse and CD-ROM drive have been installed it should be possible to run the Setup program on the Windows 95/98/Me installation disc. If the PC was booted using a Startup disc, this command is all that is needed:

setup

If the PC was booted using another boot-up disc the CD-ROM's drive letter must be specified in the command. For example, if the CD-ROM is drive D:, this command would be used:

D:\setup

After a welcome message on the screen the Scandisk utility will be run, and it will check for errors on the hard disc drives and any logical drives. Assuming all is well a screen like Figure 5.1 will appear. Press the "x" key to exit Scandisk and (if necessary) operate the Enter key to remove the onscreen message and go into the first screen of the Windows Setup program (Figure 5.2). It is then a matter of following the on-screen prompts to complete the Windows installation, providing the information that is requested, as described in the next section.

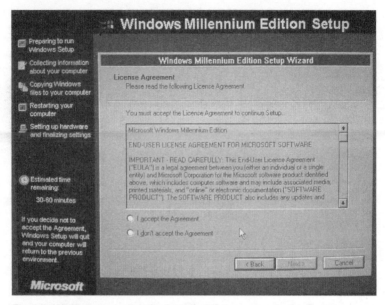

*Fig.5.3 Windows can only be installed if you agree to the licence
conditions*

Note that you can install the upgrade version of Windows 95, 98 or Me
onto a "clean" hard disc, and that it is not essential to load your old
version of Windows first so that you have something to upgrade.
However, during the installation process you will probably be asked to
prove that you have a qualifying upgrade product by putting the Setup
disc into the floppy drive or CD-ROM drive, as appropriate. Do not
throw away or recycle your old Windows discs, as this could leave you
unable to reinstall the Windows upgrade.

Installation

First you have to agree to the licensing conditions (Figure 5.3), and it is
not possible to install Windows unless you do. At the next screen the
Windows Product Key has to be entered (Figure 5.4). This code number
will be found on the Windows certificate of authenticity and (or) on the
back of the CD's jewel case. Next you are asked to select the directory
into which Windows will be installed (Figure 5.5), but unless there is
good reason to do otherwise, simply accept the default (C:\Windows).

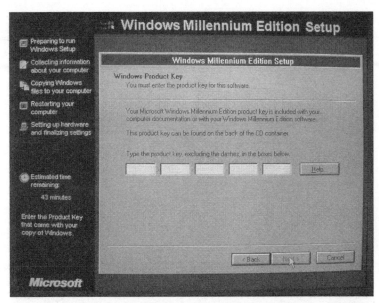

Fig.5.4 With an installation "from scratch" the product key is required

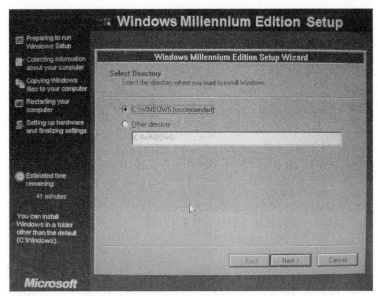

Fig.5.5 It is normally best to install Windows in the default folder

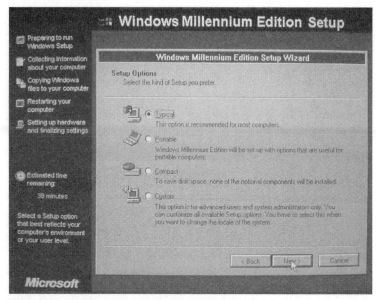

Fig.5.6 Four types of installation are available

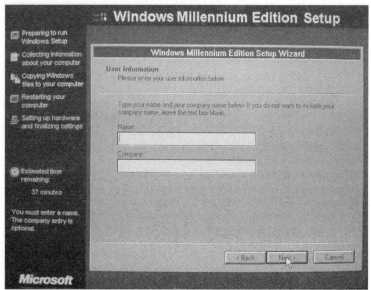

Fig.5.7 You must enter your name, but the company name is optional

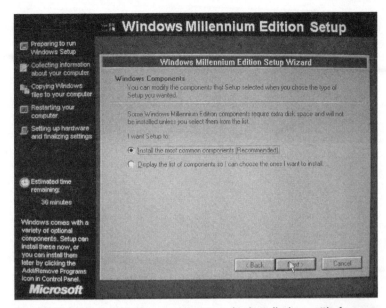

Fig.5.8 You can select the components to be installed or settle for a standard set of the most common ones

After some checking of the hard disc you are offered several installation options (Figure 5.6), but for most users the default option of a Typical installation will suffice. Remember that you can add and delete Windows components once the operating system is installed, so you are not tied to the typical installation forever.

The Custom option enables the user to select precisely the required components, but this can be time consuming and you need to know what you are doing. The Compact option is useful if hard disc space is limited, but with a new PC the hard disc will presumably be large enough to make this option superfluous. The Portable option is optimised for portable PCs, and is the obvious choice if you are installing the system on a computer of this type.

At the next screen you type your name and company name into the dialogue boxes (Figure 5.7). If an individual owns the PC the box for the company name can be left blank. The purpose of the next screen (Figure 5.8) is to let you choose the Windows components to be installed, but you can simply select a standard set of components if preferred. Operating the Next button may bring up a network identification screen

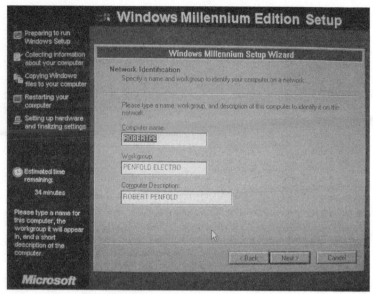

Fig.5.9 The network selection screen is not relevant to most users

(Figure 5.9). Where appropriate, make sure that this contains the correct information. In most cases the PC will not be used on a network, and the default settings can be used.

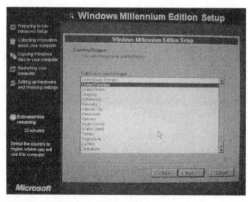

Fig.5.10 This country selection screen

Next the appropriate country has to be selected from a list (Figure 5.10), and then the required time zone is selected (Figure 5.11). This screen also provides the option of automatically implementing daylight saving changes. The next screen (Figure 5.12) enables a Windows Startup disc to be

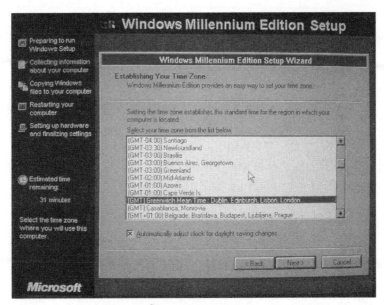

Fig.5.11 This screen is used to select the correct time zone

produced. If you already have one of these you may prefer to skip this section by operating the Cancel button and then the OK button. Unfortunately, floppy discs are not the most reliable of storage mediums. If you only have one Startup disc already, I would suggest that you go ahead and make another one so that you have a standby copy.

If you are using an upgrade version of Windows there will be an additional section in the setting up procedure where you have to prove that you have a qualifying product to upgrade from. The screen of Figure 5.13 will appear, so that you can point the Setup program towards the disc that contains the earlier version of Windows. To do this you will have to remove the upgrade disc from the CD-ROM drive and replace it with the disc for the previous version of Windows. Then either type the path to the CD-ROM drive in the text box (e.g. E:\) or operate the Browse button and point to the appropriate drive in standard Windows fashion. It takes some time for the program to check the Windows installation disc, but the program keeps you informed of its progress (Figure 5.14). Note that this stage will be passed over if you are reinstalling an upgrade version on top of an existing Windows installation. Windows will find the existing installation and will deduce from this that you are a bona fide user.

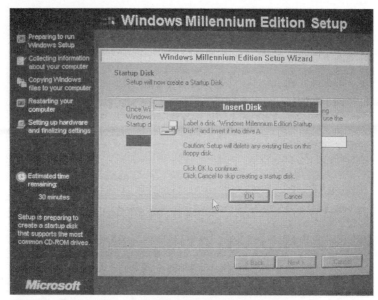

Fig.5.12 There is the option of making a Windows Startup

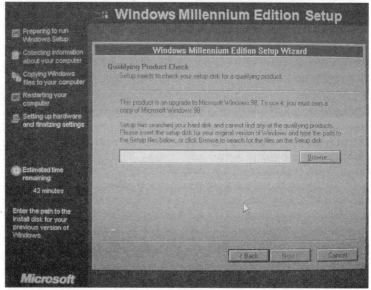

Fig.5.13 An upgrade product requires evidence of a previous version

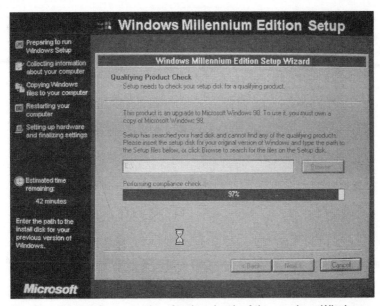

Fig.5.14 It can take some time for the check of the previous Windows installation disc to be completed, but the program keeps you informed of its progress

Having completed all this you will have finally progressed to the main installation screen (Figure 5.15), and from thereon installation is largely automatic. A screen showing how the installation is progressing will appear (Figure 5.16). The computer will reboot itself two or three times during the installation process, so if you opted to produce a Windows Startup disc during the initial set up procedure remember to remove this from the floppy drive.

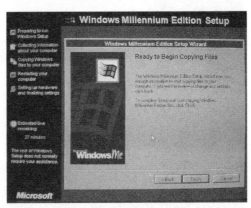

Fig.5.15 The main installation screen

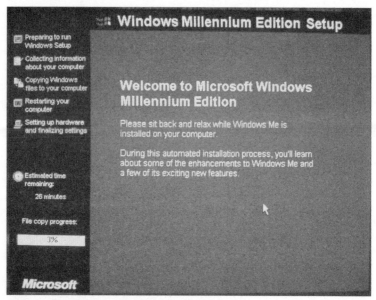

Fig.5.16 Eventually the installation begins

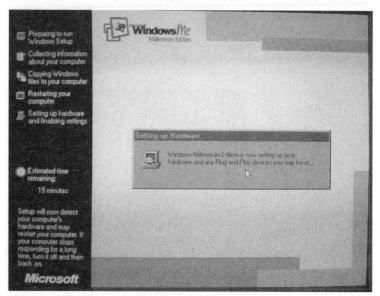

Fig.5.17 The Setup program keeps you informed of what it is doing

Otherwise the computer might reboot from the floppy rather than the hard disc, which would interfere with the installation process.

Fig.5.18 The password is optional

In the later stages of the installation there will be further screens telling you what the computer is doing, and giving an indication of how far things have progressed (Figure 5.17). No input is required from the user during all this, so you can let the computer get on with the installation. The one exception is that near the end of the installation process you will be asked to supply a user name and password (Figure 5.18). Simply leave the password text box blank if you do not require password protection. Eventually you should end up with a basic Windows installation, and the familiar initial screen (Figure 5.19).

Sometimes the Windows Setup program comes to a halt. Either the computer shows no signs of any disc activity for some time, or there may be repeated disc activity with the installation failing to make any progress. The usual cure is to switch off the computer, wait a few seconds, and then switch on again. The Setup program will usually detect that there was a problem, and will avoid making the same mistake again. If the computer is switched on and off on several occasions, but the

Fig.5.19 With installation complete the familiar Windows screen appears

installation still fails to complete, it will be necessary to reboot using the Startup disc, wipe the hard disc clean, and try again. If Windows repeatedly refuses to install it is likely that the PC has a hardware fault.

Hardware drivers

There will probably still be a certain amount of work to be done in order to get all the hardware fully installed, the required screen resolution set, and so on. Windows 95/98/Me might have built-in support for all the hardware in your PC such as the sound and video cards, but this is unlikely. In order to get everything installed correctly you will probably require the installation discs provided with the various items of hardware used in the PC. These discs may be required during the installation of Windows 95/98/Me, or they may have to be used after the basic installation has been completed. The instruction manuals provided with the hardware should explain the options available and provide precise installation instructions.

These days even the motherboards seem to come complete with driver software for things such as special chipset features and the hard disc interface. It is once again a matter of reading the instruction manual to determine which drivers have to be installed, and how to go about it. Get all the hardware properly installed before you install the applications software.

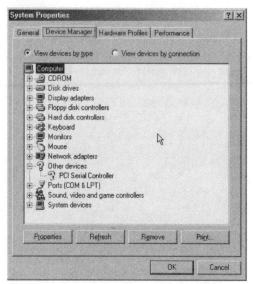

Once everything is supposedly installed correctly it is a good idea to go into the Control Panel program and double-click the System icon. Then select the Device Manager tab to bring up a window of the type shown in

Fig.5.20 Device Manager is used to check for hardware that needs further installation

Figure 5.20. Look down the various entries to check for any problems. These are indicated by yellow exclamation marks, or possibly by yellow question marks. Certain items of hardware will not be picked up properly by Windows, and some types of modem fall into this category. The question mark in Figure 5.20 is caused by a Windows modem that the system is unable to sort out on its own. A Windows modem uses a relatively simple hardware plus software in the computer to provide the encoding and decoding. Unlike a conventional modem, a Windows modem does not interface to the computer via a true serial port. It is interfaced via a sort of pseudo serial port, and it is this factor that makes it difficult to correctly identify the hardware.

If a problem is indicated, or an item of hardware is missing from the list, it will be necessary to load the drivers for the hardware concerned in order to get things working properly. This would be a good time to search the relevant web sites for updated driver software for the hardware in your PC. You may well find some newer and better drivers for the hardware in your PC. The hardware can be integrated into Windows using the Add New Hardware facility in the Control Panel. However, many items of PC hardware do not take the standard Windows route and have special installation programs instead. Read the installation manuals carefully and use the exact methods described therein.

Awkward hardware

Any awkward hardware will have to be added via the Add New Hardware facility without utilizing Windows hardware detection facility. First Windows tries to detect Plug and Play devices, and then it can try to find non-Plug and Play hardware. Failing that, the new hardware has to be installed manually using the drivers disc or discs provided with the item of hardware. The process is slightly different depending on the version of Windows

Fig.5.21 The initial Add New Hardware screen

you are using, but the basic process is the same with all three versions. Here we will consider the Windows Me version.

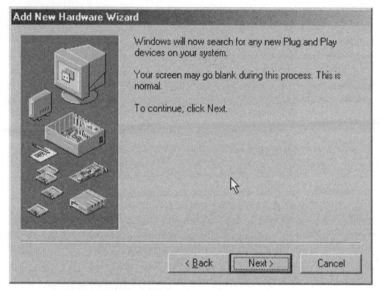

Fig.5.22 A search for Plug and Play devices is made first

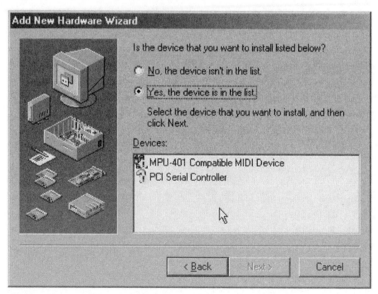

Fig.5.23 Any Plug and Play devices that are found are listed

The opening screen of Figure 5.21 appears when the Add New Hardware program is run. Heed the warning and close any programs that are running before proceeding further. To continue left-click on the Next button, which will bring up a screen like the one in Figure 5.22. This informs you that the program will look for Plug and

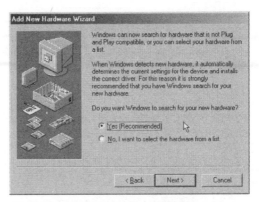

Fig.5.24 A search can be made for non-Plug and Play devices

Play devices connected to the system, and not to panic if the screen goes blank for a time. Press the Next button to proceed with the search. Eventually you will get a screen something like the one in Figure 5.23, complete with a list of any Plug and Play devices that have been found.

If the device you wish to install is in the list, leave the Yes radio button checked, left-click on the device you wish to install, and then operate the Next button to proceed with the installation.

Any non-Plug and Play devices will not be in the list, and it is then a matter of checking the No radio button and operating the Next

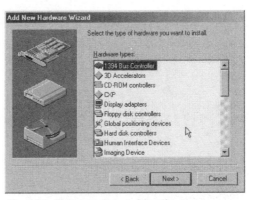

Fig.5.25 This screen enables the type of device to be selected manually

button. This brings up the window of Figure 5.24, which provides the option of having the program search for the hardware you wish to install. There is no harm in letting the program search for the hardware, although this can be quite time consuming. It is likely that a standard item of

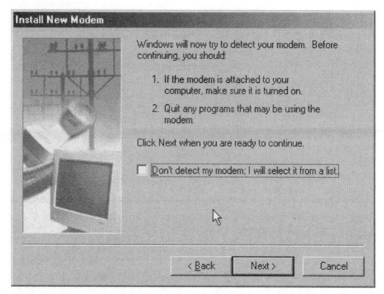

Fig.5.26 Even at this stage, automatic detection is still possible

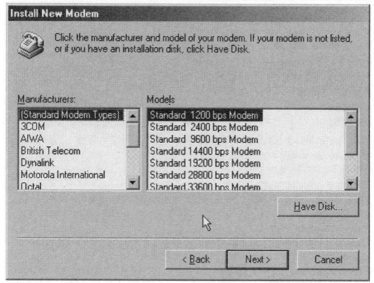

Fig.5.27 The Have Disk option is used if you have a drivers disc

hardware such as an additional serial or parallel port will be detected, but it is by no means certain that anything exotic will be located.

If you decide not to opt for automatic detection, check the No radio button and operate the Next button. This produces the window of Figure 5.25 where you can select the appropriate category for the hardware you are installing. A wide variety of devices are covered, with more available under the "Other" category. In this example the modem category was selected, and operating the Next button moved things on to the window of Figure 5.26. Here you are once again offered the option of automatic detection, but this does not work properly with most "soft" modems, so the No button was checked and the Next button was operated.

If you opt for manual selection you will eventually be shown a window containing a list of devices, as in Figure 5.27. The right device might appear in the list, but with recent hardware or generic devices you will probably be out of luck. It is then a matter of selecting the Have Disk option, which brings up a file browser so that you can direct the program to the correct disc drive, and where appropriate, the correct folder of the disc in that drive. With the drivers installed the computer will probably have to be rebooted before the hardware will operate properly.

Screen settings

Once the video card has been installed properly the required screen parameters can be set. To alter the screen resolution and colour depth, go to the Windows Control Panel and double-click on the Display icon. Then left-click on the Settings tab to bring up a screen of the type shown in Figure 5.28. It is then just a matter of using the onscreen controls to set the required screen resolution and colour depth. To use the new settings left-click the Apply button. It may be necessary to let the computer reboot in order to use the new settings, but in most cases they can be applied without doing this. Instead Windows will apply the new settings for a few seconds so that you can see that all is well. Simply left-click on the Yes button to start using the new screen settings.

If there is a problem with the picture stability do nothing, and things should return to the original settings after a few seconds. This should not really happen if the monitor is installed correctly, because Windows will not try to use scan rates that are beyond the capabilities of the installed monitor. If a problem of this type should occur, check that the monitor is installed properly. In the Display window of Control Panel select Settings, Advanced, and then Monitor. This will bring up a screen like Figure

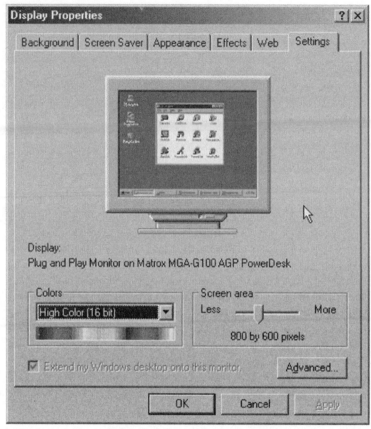

Fig.5.28 The Display Properties screen is used to set screen resolution, colour depth, etc.

5.29, which shows the type of monitor that is installed. If the installed monitor is not the correct one, or is just one of the generic monitor types, left-click the Change button and select the correct one. If the picture is stable with the new settings but the size and position are completely wrong, there is probably no problem. It should be possible to position and size the picture correctly using the monitor's controls. Many graphics cards are supplied with utility software that helps to get the best possible display from the system, and it is worth trying any software of this type to see if it gives better results.

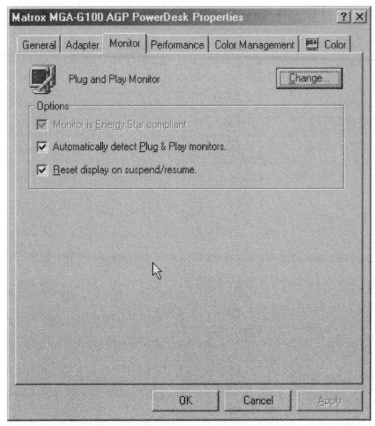

Fig.5.29 If there is screen instability check that the correct monitor is installed

Disc-free Me

It has been assumed in this chapter that you have a Windows installation CD-ROM. Some computers are supplied with Windows Me pre-installed, and they do not come complete with a Windows installation CD-ROM. Instead, the hard disc has two partitions with drive C: acting as the main disc and a much smaller drive D: containing the Windows files. There is usually a CD-ROM that can be used to recover the situation in the event of a hard disc failure, but this is not an ordinary Windows installation disc. With a computer of this type it is necessary to resort to the instruction manual for details of reinstalling Windows.

Manufacturers are able to customise the installation software to suit their PCs and any software bundled with them. Consequently there are differences in the installation procedures, but there should be a quick and easy way of getting back to a basic Windows installation. In fact some manufacturers provide a quick means of getting back to the factory settings. in other words, the computer will have Windows installed and set up correctly for the hardware installed at the factory. Of course, if you have changed the hardware configuration of the PC, it will be necessary to install the drivers for the new items of hardware.

Points to remember

Installing Windows on top of an existing version might cure problems with the operating system, but it is not guaranteed to do so.

Installing Windows "from scratch", with all the previous files removed from the hard disc should effect a cure to any Windows problems. If it does not, the computer probably has a hardware fault.

You can erase the existing Windows folder structure and then reinstall Windows. This will usually remove any problems with the original installation, but all the applications software will still have to be reinstalled.

Everything but data files can be erased from the hard disc prior to reinstalling Windows. Unless you are very unlucky, this will give a fully working Windows installation and your data files will remain intact. This method is worth trying if you have no way of backing up the data files.

Whether reinstalling Windows over an existing installation or "from scratch" it is advisable to boot from a Windows Startup disc, opting for CD-ROM support.

The basic installation process is largely automatic. The user provides some basic information and then the Setup program installs the Windows files and sets up the essential hardware. Some further installation is then required to get all the hardware properly installed, the screen resolution and colour depth set correctly, etc.

Not all hardware can be installed with the aid of the automatic detection facilities. Manual installation of hardware drivers is not difficult, but where appropriate, make sure that items of hardware are supplied complete with a disc or discs containing the driver software. Some hardware has its own installation routines and does not go through the normal Windows routes. Always install hardware in accordance with the manufacturer's instructions.

PCs that are supplied with Windows Me preinstalled are not necessarily supplied with a normal Windows installation disc. Windows then has to be installed in accordance with the computer manufacturer's instructions. The exact method of reinstallation varies somewhat from one manufacturer to another.

Appendix 1

Tweak UI

Tweak UI is a Microsoft program for making changes to the user interface. Changes that would otherwise require editing of the Registry can be made using this utility. It was originally supplied as part of the Windows 95 Power Toys package, which was a free but unsupported set of utilities.

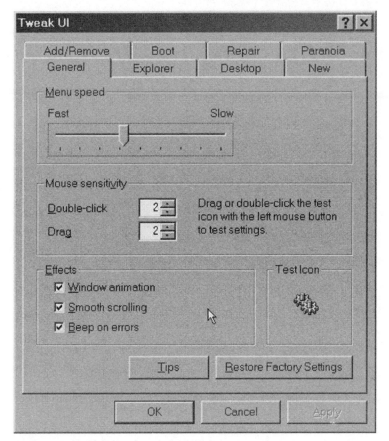

Fig.6.1 The opening screen of the Tweak UI program

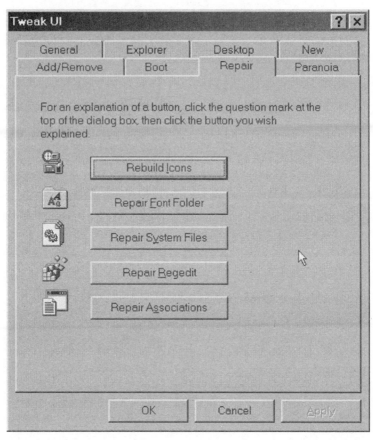

Fig.6.2 Tweak UI can repair various types of Windows fault, including some problems with the system files

It proved to be very popular, and was included as an optional extra on the original Windows 98 installation CD-ROMs. It can be found in the \Tools\reskit\powertoy folder, but note that it was omitted from the Windows 98 SE CD-ROM. It does not seem to be included with Windows Me either. For a time it was not available as a download from the Microsoft web site, but Power Toys, complete with Tweak UI, has since made a comeback. In fact the new version is bigger and better than ever.

There is no Setup program to install Tweak UI. Instead, use Windows Explorer to find the file called Tweakui.inf, right-click click on its entry and then select Install from the pop-up menu. Having installed Tweak UI there is no apparent way to run it! However, if you go to the Control Panel there should be an icon for it there. Double clicking on the icon will bring up a window like the one of Figure 6.1. There are at least two different versions of the program, so you might find that the version you are using has more or less tabs than the one in Figure 6.1.

Tweak UI provides control over various aspects of the user interface, but in the current context the facilities provided under the Repair tab (Figure 6.2) are the most useful. The buttons that appear enable various aspects of Windows to be repaired. The Repair System Files option is perhaps the one of most interest. This will repair various system files, including some of those that are most likely to bring the boot process to a halt. In order to use this facility you simply operate the appropriate button and then reboot the computer in Normal mode. If the repair has been successful the computer will then boot straight into Normal mode.

Appendix 2

Useful web addresses

www.microsoft.com

This is the Microsoft web site, and a vast amount of Windows support is available here (see chapter 2).

www.shareware.com

A vast range of shareware, freeware, commercial demonstration software, etc., is available from this site. There are also useful links to other sites. Some useful utility programs and anti-virus software can usually be obtained from here, or via one of the links.

www.symantec.com

Symantec are the publishers of the Norton range of utilities. Their web site has demonstration versions of their programs plus some virus removal tools and general anti-virus information.

Appendix 3

Regclean

Regclean is a freely obtainable utility program from Microsoft that can be used to scan the Registry for errors. Any that are found can then be fixed. Unfortunately, Regclean is not guaranteed to give perfect results every time, and under certain circumstances it can add problems rather than remove them. If you decide to give this program a try it would definitely be advisable to read the text file or files that accompany it.

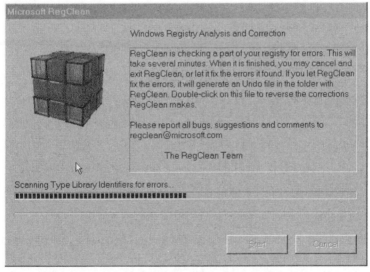

Fig.7.1 Regclean starts to operate as soon as it is launched

Also, I would not recommend it as an initial means of trying to cure problems with Windows. Just the opposite in fact, and it is probably best to leave Regclean until other avenues of investigation have been exhausted.

In order to run Regclean either use the Run option from the Start menu to run the Regclean.exe program file, or locate this file using Windows Explorer and double-click on its entry. It starts to operate immediately,

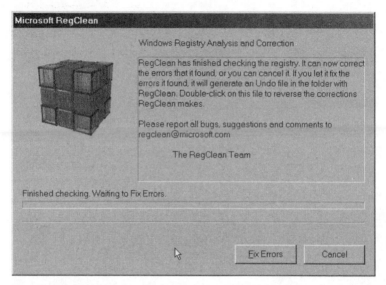

Fig.7.2 Regclean be be used to correct any errors it finds

with a check being made of various parts of the Registry (Figure 7.1). The window of Figure 7.2 appears if any errors are found, but you can operate the Exit button to quite the program without fixing them. Alternatively, operate the Fix Errors button and the suspected errors will be corrected. The window of Figure 7.3 should then appear, confirming that the errors have been fixed. Of course, there is no guarantee that any problems will be found, but Regclean usually seems to find at least one or two discrepancies. If no errors are found, the screen of Figure 7.4 appears.

If things should go badly wrong and Regclean adds rather than removes problems, there is an easy solution to the problem. When Regclean fixes errors it produces an undo file which is placed in the same folder as the Regclean.exe program file. This file has a quite a long name, but it is easily located because it starts with "Undo" and has a "Reg" extension. In order to undo the changes to the Registry locate the Undo.....Reg file using Windows Explorer and then double-click on its entry. A message will appear onscreen, asking if you wish to undo the changes to the Registry. Left-click the Yes button if you wish to proceed. The changes will then be made and a further message will appear onscreen confirming that the undo operation was successful.

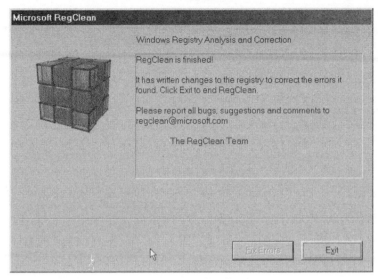

Fig.7.3 Having fixed the errors, Regclean reports that it has
completed its task

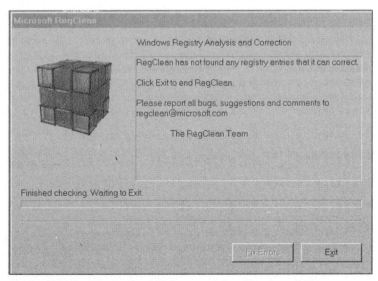

Fig.7.4 This screen appears in the event that Regclean finds
nothing amiss

Index